Malta

and its islands

Miller Distributors Limited

Miller House, Tarxien Road, Airport Way, Luqa Malta.
P. O. Box 25 Malta International Airport LQA 05
Telephone: 664488 Facsimile: 676799

MILLER

CENTRO STAMPA EDITORIALE

plurigraf

PERSEUS

Index

Text: Aldo E. Azzopardi.
Photos: Archivio Plurigraf -
Kevin Casha - Daniel Borg -
Jonathan Beacom & Perfecta Advertising.

© Copyright by CASA EDITRICE PERSEUS collection PLURIGRAF
Published and printed by Centro Stampa Editoriale, Sesto Fiorentino, (Fi).

Malta

The land and the people

Lying 90 km to the south of Sicily and 290 km to the north of the African mainland, 1830 km to the east of Gibraltar and 1500 km to the west of Alexandria, Malta and its islands might be said to occupy a position in the center of the Mediterranean.

The group is composed of the islands of Malta, Gozo and Comino all of which are inhabited, and the smaller uninhabited islands of Cominotto, Filfia and St. Paul.

The total area of the archipelago is 320 km². The longest distance in Malta in a south-east/north-west axis is about 27 km and the widest distance is 14 km. The corresponding figures for Gozo are 14 km and 7 km. Comino, the smallest of the inhabited islands being 2.6 km². The length of the shoreline around Malta is 136 km and that of Gozo is 43 km. The indentations around the coast form bays, sandy beaches and rocky coves and, more importantly, deep natural harbours.

With a population of around 350,000 crowding an area of 320 km² the Maltese Islands can claim to be the most densely populated country in Europe.

As a result of intermarriages throughout the ages, Semitic, Latin, Rhodian-Greek and a dash of Anglo-Saxon blood has produced a rich diversity of the Maltese physical "type" and it is only where character is concerned that there is conformity. Perhaps because of his fear of being swallowed up in the crowd, the average Maltese will assert his individuality by adding his personal touch to his car, boat, house or any other of his possessions. The Maltese are realists, they grumble about everything as a matter of form but they are not unduly depressed by adversity; they are blessed with the inherent ability to adjust themselves to practically any condition. The Maltese are more clannish than patriotic, in fact the awareness of a national identity arrived rather late in Malta.

To the uninformed the Maltese language sounds much like Arabic, but like most over-simplifications this statement would not be correct. The Maltese language is basically Phoenician, therefore Semitic in origin, as can be deduced from its grammar.

Arab influence in Malta lasted for more than 300 years and during that period it is inevitable that the language was enriched by many Arabic words. Moreover, some of the Sicilian loan-words are, themselves, of Arab origin. Notwithstanding the fact that the Maltese language is Semitic in origin it is written in Roman characters.

The two official languages of Malta are Maltese and English but most Maltese can also speak Italian.

The Maltese are predominantly Roman Catholic; the tangible evidence of their faith - magnificent cathedrals and churches - being the hubs and pride of every town and village.

Prehistory

At a point in time around 4,000 BC a group of Late Stone-Age Sicilian farming families left their island home to settle in a small group of islands to the south. They brought over with them their domestic animals, pottery, bags of seeds and flint implements.

They were the first Maltese.

In time more of these farmers crossed over to join the first settlers and before long little settlements dotted the islands. On occasion they returned to Sicily to obtain flint for their tools and red ochre for the funeral ceremonies as these could not be found in their new homeland.

The islands were then covered with forests and the soil was generous, while hunting and fishing added to their store of food.

In time these early Maltese increased and prospered and gang of workers could now be spared from the day to day chores so tha they could give all of their time to the building of the temples.

As the centuries rolled on the temples became more elaborate and imposing as befitted the now more prosperous communities. By this time (circa 2100 BC) new immigrants swelled the islands' population. These were more refined than their forerunners and the latest additions to the old temples were decorated with graceful spiral and animal bas-relief carvings.

The dead were now buried in a complex underground cemetery in close proximity to the temples themselves.

The new immigrants were familiar with the use of copper, although the tools they used were still being chipped out of flint as they had been for thousands of years.

Several hypotheses have been advanced to explain the presumed extinction of the temple builders: a prolonged drought; famine; epidemics and civil strife, taken in isolation or as combined causes. It is also possible that a more prosaic cause was the gradual degeneration of the race as the exhausted land could no longer support the growing population. At one time it was believed that the temple builders succumbed to an invasion of fresh migrants who exterminated, or enslaved, the original settlers and took over the land. The invasion theory cannot be entirely ruled out and still has its adherents. If there was an invasion, the new arrivals, who, originally, hailed from the heel of Italy would have had no difficulty in overcoming the remnants of the original stock who colonized the islands some 2,200 years before.

If the first settlers were peaceful farmers (no trace of weapons of the period has been discovered) the newcomers were more belligerent; these newcomers, invaders if you like, used obsidian to tip their arrows and armed themselves with bronze daggers and axes; moreover, they chose their settlement sites with care and defended them by means of stone bastions of Mycenaean proportions. These bronze-age farmers, there is some evidence to show that they were also pastoralists, were less civilized than the folk they had supplanted; they built no temples but re-used the older, copper-age, temples as cemeteries; their dead were cremated within the walls and the ashes were deposited in the ruins of the once hallowed buildings. At Tarxien one can still see the marks of their funeral pyres against the ancient walls. At times the ashes of the dead were deposited underneath dolmens, examples of which may be seen in several parts of the islands.

The bronze-age farmers were not allowed to enjoy their islands in peace because after some 600 years of their arrival a new wave of bronze-using warriors invaded the land, and this time it was definitely an invasion, and made it their home. This event took place around 1,200 BC. Like that of their predecessors, the pottery they produced was also very crude; again, these people built no temples and it is surmised that their gods were sky gods that did not require an earthly abode. Imitating their warlike predecessors, they established their settlements in easily defensible positions. Many of these settlements would have vanished without trace except for the evidence of a number of rock-hewn storage pits and the ubiquitous "cart ruts" that converge on these settlement sites. There is no satisfactory explanation for these deep, straight, parallel ruts, visible on exposed rock surfaces. It is not known what sort of vehicle caused them but it is likely that "slide-cars" (the travois of the North American Plains Indians) were probably used by these people to transport ordinary farm produce. The last of the three ages of antiquity - the Iron-Age - is represented in the Maltese Islands by the remains of a single settlement at Bahrija (circa 900 BC) but pottery of the Iron-Age has been found in many places elsewhere. It is not known where these people came from exactly; all that is known about them is that they co-existed peacefully with the bronze-age folk and were possibly respected, if not feared by them, for their mysterious knowledge of iron working. They produced finer pottery than their neighbours and they provide us with evidence of the earliest weaving industry of the islands in the form of numerous baked clay loom weights.

The Phoenicians

Their homeland a narrow coastal plain, and hemmed in by their enemies between the mountains and the Mediterranean, the only direction in which the Phoenicians could expand was seawards.

Starting off as fishermen and coastal sailors they gradually grew bolder and more experienced and ended up by becoming the foremost navigators of their day. From the coast of present day Lebanon and Syria, these intrepid seamen crossed the length and breadth of the Mediterranean establishing staging posts on the way.

The Maltese islands with their fine natural harbours was one such outpost which the Phoenicians founded around 800 BC. The Phoenicians were not interested in establishing an empire, all they wanted was a chain of safe harbours in which to refit and repair their vessels; they settled on the coast and hardly ever ventured far inland, they were also careful to establish and maintain a friendly rapport with the indigenous populations amongst whom they settled.

As it was in other countries, so it was in Malta: having gained a foothold as traders, they gradually intermarried and integrated with the bronze-age farmers and it was only a matter of time before they converted the inhabitants of the islands to their customs and their beliefs. This assimilation did not, of course, take place overnight, but when it eventually did happen, the new race became the rootstock of the Maltese People, and the language of these people the basis of the Maltese Language.

The larger island was now called M-L-T (Malet: meaning shelter) and the smaller island was named G-L (Gol, after the broad beamed trading vessel).

Because the Phoenicians are best known as navigators and merchants, other talents of these remarkable people are often lost sight of: the Phoenicians were not only seamen and traders but they also excelled in industry, particularly in the weaving and the dying of fine cloth, Thyrian Purple being the material of many a royal robe in antiquity; they are also credited with having invented glass.

Another achievement of these seamen/traders was systematic agricul-

ture: most of their trading outposts were, in fact, self-sufficient as far as provisions were concerned and they were responsible for the propagation of the pomegranate of which they were very fond.

The most important Phoenician remains in the Maltese Islands are those at Tas-Silg, to the south-east of Malta; these remains are much disturbed by later superimposed constructions (themselves, in a ruined state) and are still being studied.

In this period of the story of Malta we are in the realm of written history, and it is recorded that overlooking the two main harbours in Malta were famous temples dedicated to Phoenician Deities - one in what is now the Grand Harbour, probably under the foundations of Fort St.

Angelo, sacred to Melkart and another dedicated to Astarte in the aforementioned Tas-Silg area.

In the case of the Maltese Islands the Phoenicians did venture inland because their remains have been found in several places, even as far as Rabat in the center of the island of Malta.

It is not recorded what articles of trade were produced by the Phoenicians who made the Maltese islands their home but it is reasonable to assume that these items could have included olive-oil (the indigenous forests having been devastated long before by the bronze-age folk). The weaving industry that flourished before the arrival of the Phoenicians probably received an added boost and a wider export market. Pottery was

now thrown on a wheel instead of being coiled as was previously the case.

The links between the Phoenician colonies and the Mother Country were never very strong and when the Phoenician homeland was overrun it was the Phoenician colony of Carthage that took over the rôle of Mother Country so that in around 480BC we find that Phoenicians from Carthage (modern-day Tunisia) were casting their influence, rather than their control, over the islands.

These Carthaginians were very much like their Phoenician cousins who had established themselves in the Maltese Islands except that they were much more warlike and cruel. One of their goddesses was Tanit to whom babies and young chil-

dren were sacrificed in times of disaster.

There is no evidence that human sacrifices were practised in Malta at this time although the Cross of Tanit has been discovered in a Late Punic man-made cave at Dwejra, Gozo.

In many sectors of the Mediterranean littoral the Phoenicians-Carthaginians strove to establish a sphere of influence, their chief rivals in this respect being the Greeks. The Hellenes were motivated by love of empire but all that the Carthaginians wanted was to extend their outlets for foreign trade.

Surprisingly, in the Maltese Islands these differences did not seem to exist: it is not known how many Greeks lived, co-existed rather, with the Phoenicians and the Carthaginians on the Island, but some undoubtedly did - civic institutions resembled their Greek counterparts and Greek coins and pottery have been found on the islands. A number of Greek inscriptions have also been unearthed, one, in particular is of special interest: it is a dedication to Melkart in the Phoenician language followed by its Greek translation. This cippus might be termed the Maltese "Rosetta Stone" because it was instrumental in deciphering the Phoenician language by an 18th Century scholar.

By this time the Maltese were no longer "isolated"; situated, as they were, in the cross-roads of shipping lanes, Malta and its islands were a center of activity: the repair, and possibly the building of ships, the production of fine linen cloth, olive-oil and honey and, not least, catering for the pilgrims who came to worship in the temples by the harbours which were then famous in many lands. Ancient Egyptian amulets of the period have been discovered in the temple sites.

Unfortunately the islands were also a venue for other sea-farers - the pirates - despite the presence of the formidable Carthaginian war- galleys that patrolled the Mediterranean, piratical incursions were a common occurrence, a scourge that was to last into centuries yet to come: capture, and carrying off into slavery was to be the fate of many a Maltese for a very long time.

The Romans

The three Punic Wars were to last for over a hundred years and during this struggle between the Carthaginians and the Romans, Sicily and its appendage, the Maltese islands, were to occupy central stage in the theatre of war for the control of the Mediterranean.

Initially, with their vastly superior navy, the Carthaginians had the upper hand and by this time (264BC) the Maltese harbours were an important base of the Carthaginian war galleys.

By the end of the First Punic War, in 241 BC, the whole of Sicily had been ceded to the Romans but the Carthaginians were allowed to retain the Maltese Islands.

Peace did not last long, however, because in 218 BC a second war broke out and, learning from their past mistakes, the Romans were determined to capture the islands.

Apparently the invasion did not present great difficulties and it has been suggested that the Phoenicians on the Island turned against their Carthaginian cousins and handed over the garrison to the invading Romans. Treated, at first, as a conquered territory, the Maltese Islands were administered by a Procurator who was responsible for civil and military affairs, but not long afterwards they were raised to the level of a municipality with an autonomous local government; there is also some evidence that the island of Gozo was made a Municipium in its own right. The Maltese were treated more like allies than as a conquered people which lends some substance to the "collaboration" theory. The Maltese kept their Punic traditions and language and their gods. The two larger islands were renamed Melita and Gaulos and it has been tentatively suggested that the name Melita was not a Romanized version of the Phoenician Malet, but derived from mel (honey) for which the islands were then famous (centuries later, in 70BC, Maltese delegates in Rome denounced the Roman Provincial Governor of Sicily and Malta, Caius Verres, with having stolen, inter alia, 400 jars of honey).

With Carthage destroyed in the Third Punic War, and the Greeks overcome, the Mediterranean became a Roman Lake - the Mare Nostrum, the areas of conflict of imperial conquest now being the lands bordering this sea.

At this time the Maltese Islands were relatively safe from piratical attacks and, true to Roman imperial policy, not being a frontier outpost, the islands were organised so as to be more productive in essential commodities most of which would eventually find their way to Rome, the centre of the Empire. These improvements would have included a more advanced irrigation system and cultivation methods practised on a vast scale. The most important agricultural products of the islands being, at this time, linen, honey, wax and olive-oil (olive-pitters, mills that separated the flesh of olives from their stones, being the most common finds of the period). Another important, and lucrative, industry must have been the servicing and provisioning of ships; the old harbour works were extended and new ones laid down. Evidence of such works has been unearthed at Burmarrad (a silted-up harbour) and St. Paul's Bay in Malta, and Xlendi and at Marsalforn in Gozo. The small island of Comino must have been permanently occupied from, at least, this period. Although the economy of the islands was largely rural, there was a leisured and cultured class of Maltese living here at the same time; these people emulated their Roman overlords in their way of life and evidence of their good taste can be seen in many parts of the islands in the shape of fine mosaic floors and marble statuary, all of which were imported, which would indicate a measure of opulence of these Romanized Maltese.

Some for them even made a name for themselves as philosophers and orators in Rome.

The Romans built the city of Melita, itself bearing the same name as that of the island. The city was built over an older, Punic settlement in what is now the Rabat/Medina area in Malta, and also another town in Gozo under what is now Victoria (Rabat).

Unfortunately very few remains have come to light in these areas because, from, at least, Roman time onwards they were never abandoned as places of habitation and many a mosaic floor must be lying under the foundations of houses that cover every square metre of space in these areas.

The capital cities of Melita and Gaulos were protected by walls, as sections of the defensive Roman works are occasionally exposed when an old house is knocked down, but villas were scattered all around the islands and the fact that these were situated away from the walled towns and fortifications may be taken as an indication that life and property were relatively safe and that there was a measure of stability in the land.

In one instance, at least, a round Roman tower had outlived its purpose and was, during this period, converted into a farmhouse.

In time, the old gods, too, became Romanized, so that Astoret (whose name had been sometimes Hellenized into Hera in the past) was now venerated under the Roman appelation of Juno, but the old temple, with several modifications and additions, still occupied the site overlooking Marsaxlokk harbour. Melkart became Heracles and new gods were added to the pantheon: Apollo had his temple and

so did Proserpine, the former in Rabat and the other at Mtarfa, but their locations have disappeared without trace. Other, unrecorded, temples must have also existed.

Saint Paul

The shipwreck of St. Paul in 60AD is recorded in some detail in the Acts of the Apostles, and a Pauline tradition of long standing supported by archeological excavations carried out at San Pawl Milqgħi prove beyond doubt that his arrival in Malta is a historical fact and it is also a fact that during his three-month stay on the Island he sowed the first seeds of the Christian Religion to which Maltese people overwhelmingly belong, but inevitably, a number of legends have grown up over the centuries, some verg-

ing on the impossible, but others not without a grain of truth.

The Apostle Paul was, at this time, being conducted to Rome under arrest to be judged before Caesar as was his right as a Roman Citizen. Amongst the other prisoners was the physician St. Luke who recorded the account of that eventful journey.

Leaving a harbour in Crete with the intention of making a safer harbour along the coast in which to winter, the grain ship in which they were travelling was blown off course by

the fury of the storm until, after being tossed about for fourteen days, the ship arrived at night off what is now presumed to have been Qawra Point. The sound of the breakers surging over the shallows indicated that they were close to land so that the stern anchors were lowered to keep the ship from drifting. As soon as it was light the vessel drove before the wind, around Qawra Point and into what is now St. Paul's Bay. The vessel ran aground on a spit of rock known as Tal-Għazzini - the myth that the actual spot of the shipwreck was St. Paul's Islands is a comparatively recent romantic invention.

The nearest habitation to the place of shipwreck was the villa of Publius, the Chief Man of the Island. All those who had been shipwrecked spent three days there and after they had regained their strength they moved on to Melita the chief town of the island. In the city Paul cured Publius' father of a fever after which the Chief Man of the Island was converted to Christianity and later ordained Bishop by St. Paul, St. Publius being the first bishop of Malta.

Still nominally a prisoner, St. Paul had been confined to a cave prison (now St. Paul's Grotto, Rabat) but he was still allowed ample freedom of movement which enabled him to spread his evangelistic mission and to perform many miraculous cures.

After three months, by which time, the sea was again reckoned to be safe for navigation, and loaded with gifts from his Maltese friends, Saint Paul sailed away to Rome and to his subsequent martyrdom. The village of Naxxar is supposed to be the place where St. Paul and his companions washed and dried their clothes prior to their entry into Melita and the place where the Apostle is said to have made his first converts.

On one of the outside walls of the church of Marsalforn in Gozo is recorded the pious legend that while St. Paul was preaching from what is now Rabat in Malta, the Gozitan people on that spot, some

20 km away, could hear his voice and were converted to the new Faith. A mundane explanation for the origin of this legend is that during the Roman Period Marsalforn was one of the ports of the island, and it was at this place that the Apostle landed on his first visit to that island.

With the passage of time the area surrounding St. Paul's Grotto became honeycombed with catacombs which were used as places of burial, and the shrines in them as places of worship; unlike catacombs, elsewhere, the ones in Malta were never used as places of refuge. There is no record of persecution of Christians on the islands, indeed, according to legend St. Agatha escaped to Malta from Catania around the year 250AD to escape persecution; it is also pleasant to relate that Jews, Pagans and Christians lived together in harmony in the Maltese Islands.

When the Roman Emperor Constantine embraced Christianity and made it the official religion of the Empire it may be assumed that Christian worship was better organised and that a number of places of assembly were built in various places in the islands. Tradition has it that one such church was built on the site of the palace of Publius, where St. Paul had cured the father of the Chief Man of the Island. Many times rebuilt, the site is now occupied by the Cathedral Church dedicated to Saint Paul at Mdina.

An Empire in Decline

When the Roman Empire had been divided between the two sons of the Emperor Theodosius, Malta and its islands came under the Empire of the East which had its capital in remote Byzantium (modern day Istanbul). Very little is known of Maltese history regarding the four centuries starting from around the year 400 AD. This was the period of the break-up of the old Roman Empire, the time when Vandals and Goths carried all before them in Spain and in North Africa and, in-

deed, on the Italian mainland, the City of Rome itself was taken. The Byzantines, however, were more successful in warding off the attacks of the barbarians largely because of their powerful navy.

With General Bellisarius in command, a strong Byzantine force set out to retrieve the former Roman possessions in North Africa and it is recorded that on the way the in 533AD he called at Malta but the report does not specify whether Bellisarius liberated the islands, assuming of course that such an action was necessary. Two years later Sicily was conquered.

About the middle of the 6th Century the lands under Byzantine domination were organised into a series of military provinces or Themes. The establishment of the Themes being rather similar to a general proclamation of martial law with the military in control. Towards the end of the 7th Century or the beginning of the 8th we find the name of Niceta, Drungario and Arconte of Malta, an officer of the new Byzantine military organization which in the face of the Moslem threat assumed civil and military rule. It is possible that Malta may have become a strong base for the Byzantine warships but notwithstanding this increase in activity and the war-economy it generated, living conditions, nonetheless, remained pitiable.

With the collapse of the rule of law and trade more or less at a standstill, it is most likely that the inhabitants of the islands, for the most part, gradually reverted back to a state of semi-barbarism and scratched a bare living in the shadow of the once magnificent buildings - the ruined evidence of a glorious past. Byzantine remains on the islands are, in fact, few and of a poor quality. One spark in the surrounding darkness was the fact that by this time most, if not the whole, of the population would have been converted to the Christian Faith and that for a number of Maltese, hope in a better world to come made their miserable one on earth more bearable.

The Arabs

The Gods, we are told, are unable to change the past, but this does not seem to deter historians from trying - probably no period of Maltese History is more influenced by sentiment and prejudice than the Arab Period. Latter day historians see the Maltese as being: either persecuted for remaining steadfast to their Faith, and obliged to practise their religious rites in the safe seclusion of the catacombs; or else, renouncing their religion and customs and adopting those of the Arab conquerors, lock, stock and barrel.

The Arab attacks on the islands started from around the year 836 during which time Malta and its islands were still under Byzantine rule, but the islands were only overcome in the year 870 by Aglabid Arabs originating from what is now Tunisia who used Sicily as a springboard for their invasion, that island having been occupied by them some thirty years previously.

The Christian forces fought hard to defend the islands but in the end they had to submit.

After the Arabs had occupied Malta, the Maltese were probably not treated very harshly by their conquerors; as People of the Book (i.e. of the Bible) they, together with the Jews then on the island, were beyond the pale of paganism that was anathema to the followers of the Prophet. Islam now supplanted Christianity as the state religion and certain restrictions were imposed on those of the latter creed. Those Jews and Christians who would not declare that Mohammed was the Prophet of God were obliged to pay a tribute, the harag, and such people were treated as dimmi, or second-class citizens, but there probably was never any persecution as such. From the census ordered by the Emir, in the year 991 it appears that the number of Christian families was 6,339 while that of Moslem families was recorded as being 14,972. Such figures would seem to be out of proportion to the Arab remains found locally; it is significant that only the remains of a single mosque of the period have been found. A possible explanation is that many a Maltese, in order to avoid paying the tribute, had merely acknowledged that Mohammed was the Prophet of God without renouncing their Christian religion, and thus went down as Moslem in the census.

Arabophiles, on the other hand, opt for a thorough conversion of the inhabitants and claim that any evidence of the Moslem religion was systematically destroyed by the Maltese in their religious zeal when, centuries later, they were brought back into the European and Christian fold. Any Moslem remains would have been of doubtful artistic value because during this period Sicily seems to have been a hub of Arab culture and art but the Maltese islands must have been something of a backwater in this respect.

Be that as it may, even if the number of Christians was reduced, the Christian Religion still survived and pockets of Christians, at least, co-existed with their Arab rulers. These Christians were known to the Arabs as the Rum, and a number of placenames with this connotation exist in the islands, such as Wied ir-Rum (the Valley of the Christians), near Imtahleb.

To better protect their new territories the Moslems sectioned off a part of the old Roman town of Melita and defended it with a ditch, calling this citadel Mdina, and did the same thing to the capital of the sister island, Gozo; the élite of the small number of Arabs then on the islands, probably dwelt in these towns but Arab villages were scattered on both islands; such as Bahrija in Malta (baharija: Arabic for oasis) and the village of Gharb in Gozo (gharb: Arabic for West - that hamlet being the most westerly of the Maltese Islands). The name of the two principal islands, Melita and Gaulos, were changed to Malta and Għawdex and two of the smaller islands were named Kemmuna and Filfla, named after the

cummin seed and peppercorn respectively. Besides a wealth of placenames, the Maltese Language has been enriched by many Arabic words, the organic growth of the language being facilitated, in this instance, by the process of assimilation made easier by the fact that both the Arabic and Maltese languages shared a common Semitic denominator.

The older villages with their cube-shaped, almost windowless houses, and flat roofs bear the stamp of the Arab builders, the inspirators of this style of architecture.

The Arabs introduced the water-wheel, the sienja, an animal-driven device for raising water, now practically obsolete, and, much more importantly, the cultivation of the cotton-plant, the mainstay of the Maltese economy for several centuries.

To guard the main harbour the Arabs built a fort where the Temple of Heracles once stood and under the shadow of its walls, Arab corsair vessels rode at anchor; several Maltese who had previously made their living from the sea were pressed into service on board these craft. The Byzantines made several attempts to recapture the islands and on one occasion reinforcements had to be sent over from Sicily.

Reports now reached the Arabs that the Byzantines were preparing for yet another invasion attempt.

Amongst other restrictions, the Maltese were forbidden to bear arms, a terrible mark of shame for an Arab, but far less so where the Maltese were concerned. In expectation of the invasion the Emir revoked the order, and in the words of the Arab historian, Kawzuni, declared "Take up arms on our side, if we win you shall be free like ourselves and you will share with us all we possess; if you do not fight, we shall be killed and so will you".

The Arabs, aided by the Maltese, repelled the invaders and, true to their word, the Arabs now (1048) treated the Maltese more liberally. In the meantime, away to the north, in Sicily, the Normans seemed to

be getting the best of the Arabs in the wars that had been dragging on for over a generation for the mastery of that island.

The Middle Ages

The Arabs in Sicily were divided, and taking advantage of the situation, Count Roger the Norman, after a series of compaigns, subdued that island to Norman Rule.

Count Roger was the son of a Norman condottiere who had carved out a kingdom for himself in the southern Italian Peninsula. In the popular Maltese imagination Roger is the paladin in shining armour who ousted the Saracens from the islands, restored Christian worship, and gave the Maltese their National Flag. As an historical figure this description, and that of his exploits, is not quite correct.

The same year he had occupied Sicily, in 1090, at the head of a small force, Count Roger landed in Malta and quickly overcame the weak resistance put up by the Arabs on the islands.

Count Roger had invaded the islands to make sure his southern flank was secure from a possible Arab attack, having reduced the Arabs to a state of vassalage and releasing the foreign Christian slaves, he returned to Sicily without even bothering to garrison his prize. Apparently he also left untouched the institutions that had been set up by the Arabs with the exception that no tribute was to be paid by those not of the Muslim Faith.

In Sicily itself the Normans followed the same enlightened policy and although the Christian Faith was regarded as the official religion there, nobody was persecuted because of his race or for his religious beliefs.

In 1127, Roger II the son of Count Roger, led a second invasion of Malta; having overrun the Island he placed it under a more secure Norman domination under the charge of a Norman governor, and he also garrisoned with Norman soldiers the three castles then on the

islands. From about this period the Maltese moved back gradually into the European orbit to which they had belonged for a thousand years prior to the Arab interlude. The Christian consolidation must have come later because Bishop Burkhard von Strassburg, ambassador of Frederick I to Saladin, remarked during his stop in the Maltese Islands, in 1175, that most of the inhabitants were Moslems.

Because the last Norman king died without a male heir, the new masters of the Maltese islands came, in turn, from the ruling houses of Germany, France and Spain: the Swabians (1194); the Angevins (1268); the Aragonese (1283) and finally, the Castillians (1410).

When the Norman Period came to an end, the Fief of Malta was granted to loyal servants of the Sicilian Crown; these Counts, or Marquises of Malta, as these nobles were styled, looked on the fief simply as an investment - a source for the collection of taxes and something that was bartered or sold when no

longer viable. The Maltese people wished to have the Island included in the Royal Domains under the direct rule of the Sovereign rather than under the rule of the grasping feudal counts. Following several representations, their request for an incorporation was granted on a number of occasions, but none of these permanent incorporations lasted for any length of time. About the time of the first incorporation, in 1350, the first Maltese Nobles were created and, not long afterwards, the Maltese elected council and its administrative body, the Università were officially recognised by the king. The Island of Gozo likewise had its own municipal government. The king also created the post of Governor who was chosen from among the members of the Council; officially known as the Capitano di Verga, he was referred to as the Hakem by the Maltese, that title being the Arab designation for that official. Following an Arab uprising in Sicily, Frederick II, ruler of Germany and Sicily

had the Arabs expelled from all his territories in 1249, and although some of the Moslems might have converted to the Christian Faith, and, in this way, avoided eviction, others probably left the Island, their places being taken over by immigrants from Sicily.

During this period the City States of Pisa, Genoa and Venice were the foremost maritime powers of the Mediterranean and now that the Arab incursion in that sea had been stemmed and, eventually, the Arabs forced to retreat, the trading vessels of these Italian states, protected by their respective navies, opened up trade routes that brought to the countries of Europe merchandise from Egypt and the Near East. These maritime states, at times, allied themselves to the masters of the Maltese Islands, and at other times to their enemies.

Piracy was still a flourishing occupation for the inhabitants of the islands but it was a risky occupation in more ways than one: beside the dangers encountered on the high seas, a successful attack and the capture of a foreign vessel sometimes resulted in a retaliatory attack by the injured party as happened in 1371 when ten Genoese vessels attacked, and laid waste the islands.

The Maltese were now drawn more closely into the Sicilian orbit and they came to depend on the nearby island for most of their necessities, particularly corn and livestock.

The last feudal lord of Malta, Don Gonsalvo Monroy, had been expelled from the Island following a revolt and at the Court of Sicily the count demanded that the strongest measures be taken against the insurgents. At the same Court the representatives of the Maltese offered to repay the 30,000 florins originally paid by Monroy for the Fief of Malta; they also asked for the Island to be incorporated in the Royal Domains once they had redeemed their homeland. The king, Alphonse V, impressed by their loyalty, called Malta the most notable gem in his crown, thus the capital of Malta came to be called Notabile although, then, as now, the Maltese continued to call the town Mdina.

It was agreed that the sum of money was to be repaid within four months but when the viceroy, Nicola Speciali, visited the island and saw for himself that the cotton crop had failed and the miserable state the inhabitants were in, he extended the period of payment.

On his deathbed in 1429, Monroy pardoned the Maltese the sum of 10,000 florins still owing to him.

By this time, the Maltese were thoroughly Christianized and the houses of the great Religious Orders were being established in the Island: the Franciscans (1370); the Carmelites (1418); the Augustinians (1450); the Dominicans (1466); and the Minor Observants (1492), while the Benedictine Sisters arrived in 1418.

It was the members of these Orders who started the first elementary schools, promising scholars then went to Sicily to pursue their higher education. The first hospital services were also among the works of mercy of these friars.

The defence of the islands rested largely on the shoulders of the Maltese themselves. Backed by a small garrison of foreign soldiers, the miilitia companies, known as the Dejma, were enrolled from the entire population on a roster basis, all males between the ages of sixteen and sixty being obliged to serve; during times of emergency, older and younger persons were also liable to be called up.

Living under the threat of surprise corsair attacks, and at the risk of being carried off into slavery, was a way of life the Maltese had to contend with for many centuries.

Town houses belonging to this period may be seen at Mdina and at the Citadel, Victoria in Gozo generally, and wrongly, described as being in the Norman Style. Country chapels of the same period are those of is-Sincier near Rabat, and Hal Millieri, near Zurrieq. A number of underground chapels could also have been in use during this period; an outstanding example being that of the Church/Crypt of St. Agatha, again at Rabat.

In 1429 a determined attempt was made by an army of 18,000 Moors from Tunisia under Kaid Ridavan to capture the Maltese islands with the intention of using them as an advance post for further conquests. The Maltese population then numbered between 16,000 to 18,000 with only some 4,000 men under arms. The invaders were beaten back but not before they had captured over 3,000 of the inhabitants as prisoners.

The details of that epic defence are largely unknown, but some stories have come down to us in folk tales and in ballads; it is told that the Moors, as a sign that they intended to overcome the Maltese by force of arms and that they did not intend to reduce the defenders by starvation, sent the besieged a waggonload of bread, upon which, the Maltese defenders sent back the waggon with a gbejna (the typical small Maltese cheeselet) on each loaf!

According to another legend, St. Paul appeared in the sky riding a white horse and brandishing a sword, and it was this vision that scared off the Moors when they practically had the Island in their grasp. And this was not to be the last occasion when the Maltese were to call upon their Patron Saint to save them from the fury of the corsairs.

The Knights of the Order of St. John

The visitor arriving by air will probably first notice it in the livery colours of Air Malta, the national airline; he will see it again and again during his stay on the Island: carved on the façade of Baroque palaces, in the form of exquisite filigree brooches, and embossed on many a kitsch, plastic souvenir. It is the eight-pointed cross, or, as it is better known, the Maltese Cross.

This cross, a white emblem over the black habit of the Benedictine Monks, was originally worn by a dedicated band of volunteers who bound themselves to help sick and weary pilgrims in the Holy Land. The monks were then known as the Hospitallers of St. John of Jerusalem, a religious order confirmed as such by Pope Pascal II in the year 1113. Not long afterwards the need was felt to protect pilgrims on the route to their destination and in this way, the Order became, in addition, a Military Order of knights. By the middle of the 12th Century the order was headed by a Grand Master, its members coming from the noblest houses in Christendom.

As a military order, the Knights took part in the crusading wars, but when Acre fell in 1291, they were driven off from their last stronghold in the Holy Land.

After a short stay in Cyprus, the Knights, with the assistance of the Genoese, occupied Rhodes. This was to be their home for the next two hundred years.

In Rhodes the Knights perfected the base for their organization that was to make them the most efficient sea-borne warriors of their day. From the island of Rhodes, the Knights harassed the shipping of the Ottoman Empire and even dared engage the Turks on their own territories. In 1522 the Sultan Suleiman laid siege to Rhodes and after a heroic resistance that lasted six months, the Knights were forced to surrender and were again without a home.

After wandering for seven years the Knights, and the Rhodian refugees who had attached themselves to them, were offered the Island of Malta for a home by the Holy Roman Emperor, Charles V, with Tripoli as an added, unwelcome, bonus. The nominal yearly rent was the presentation of a falcon to the Viceroy of Sicily.

When the Knights arrived in Malta in 1530 they had a mixed reception: the common people hoped that under the Order they would be better protected against corsair attacks; on the other hand, the notables of the Island viewed the arrival of the Knights as an infringement of the promise that the Island would not be given in fief, although by this time the islanders had learned that it was futile to put one's trust in the promises of princes. During the ceremonial entry into the city the aged Grand Master swore that he would uphold the rights and privileges of the Maltese people. And Malta entered into the most glorious period of its history. At this time the Knights hoped that the stay on the island would be of short duration as they were still hoping to reconquer Rhodes, but as time passed and the prospect of that happening grew dimmer, the Knights prepared to settle in their new home.

The chief, possibly, the only, attraction that the Island held for the Knights, was its fine harbours, and now that the Order was more of a naval, than a land force, the Knights came to appreciate the advantage of these secure havens for their galleys.

To the relief of the Maltese Nobles, the Knights decided that Mdina, the capital city, was too far inland and they set about establishing themselves in the small village that had grown up behind the old Castel à Mare. This ancient castle they repaired and renamed St. Angelo; they also built a small fort on the tip of the peninsula that separated the two main harbours and named it St. Elmo. In Birgù the Knights organized themselves along the lines they had evolved during their stay in Rhodes. Their philanthropic origin was not forgotten and amongst the first buildings to be set up was a hospital.

The Order could be described as a multi-national force divided into Langues according to the nationality of its members, these langues, or tongues, were: Auvergne, Provence, France, Aragon, Castile, England, Germany and Italy. Each langue had its own Auberge, or headquarters, as well as a specific duty traditionally assigned to it; each langue was also responsible for the defence of a particular post, such as a section of a bastion or tower.

As if to prove the inadequacy of the defences of the islands in 1547, and again in 1551, the Turks launched two attacks against the islands, the latter being particularly calamitous. Ravaging the Maltese countryside and ignoring the fortified towns, the Turks then turned their attention to the island of Gozo and carried away the entire population into slavery.

That same year the Turks drove the Knights out of Tripoli. These attacks stung the Knights into feverish activity to improve the islands' defences in anticipation of another, and possibly bigger, attack.

At the same time the galleys of the Order, at times aided by those of Maltese corsairs, never ceased from their attacks on Ottoman shipping and on the vassal territories on the North African coast, which attacks made the Turks more determined than ever to drive the Knights out of their latest home.

The Great Siege

"Nothing is better known than the siege of Malta" wrote Voltaire two hundred years after the event, and for the Maltese people today the statement still rings true. For the Maltese people the Great Siege was, in Churchillian phrase, their finest hour.

The bare bones of the narrative are as follows:

On the 18th May, 1565, the Ottoman Turks and their allies pitted 48,000 of their best troops against the islands with the intention of invading them, and afterwards to make a thrust into Southern Europe by way of Sicily and Italy.

Against them were drawn up some 8,000 men: 540 Knights; 4,000 Maltese; and the rest made up of Spanish and Italian mercenaries.

La Valette, the Grand Master, perhaps the greatest Grand Master the Order ever had, wisely did not attempt to meet the invaders on the beaches, but chose, instead, to deploy the small number of troops at his disposal inside the fortified positions: the old town of Mdina; the two fortified towns by the har-

bours, Senglea and Birgu; and St. Elmo, the small fort that had been built on the tip of the Sciberras peninsula to guard the entrances of the two main harbours. A small token force garrisoned the castle at Gozo.

Landing unopposed, the first objective of the Turks was to secure a safe anchorage for their large invasion fleet, and with that in mind, launched their attack on St. Elmo. After a heroic resistance of thirty-one days the fort succumbed to the massive bombardment and continuous attacks of the Turks. After the fort had been reduced, the Ottomans turned their attention to the two badly fortified towns overlooking the harbour. Subjected to a ceaseless bombardment, and repulsing attack after attack; behind the crumbling walls, the Christian forces, against all odds, kept the enemy at bay until a small relief force of some 8,000 troops arrived from Sicily (a smaller relief force of 600 men had previously landed at about the time that St. Elmo had fallen). Totally demoralized, as the Turks were, by losses from disease, fire and steel, added to the fact that their supplies were running low, they were in no position to offer an effective resistance, and the Turks retreated never again to attempt another invasion in that part of the Mediterranean. The Knights, the Spanish and Italian mercenaries, and the entire Maltese population, all of whom were in the front line of the fighting, had triumphed. In saving themselves, they saved Europe from the Ottoman Turks.

Praise, and what was more important, aid, poured from the grateful Christian princes of Europe. And plans, long shelved, were unrolled. Malta was to have a new city, a city whose ramparts would last as long as time.

The Foundation of Valletta

The idea of fortifying the rocky and steep-sided Mount Sciberras had occured to the Knights on their arrival in 1530, but because time was not on their side, they limited themselves to building a fort at its very tip, instead.

If other Grand Masters studied the possibilities of such a project, La Valette was obsessed with the idea; as soon as he had been elected to the Grand Mastership in 1557 he invited foreign military engineers, famous in their time, to prepare the plans, but the Great Siege put a stop to all that. No sooner was the siege lifted than the plans for the fortress city were again revived, but as a first step the ill-fated Fort St. Elmo was at once rebuilt.

Pope Pius IV sent his military engineer, Francesco Laparelli, and the planning of the new town started in earnest.

The foundation stone was laid on the 28th March 1566 with the pomp that befitted such an undertaking, and the new city named Valletta after the Grand Master.

Soon afterwards the whole work force of the Island was deployed on the project.

In fear of Turkish reprisal raids, priority was given to the building of the bastions and the cutting of a ditch which was to isolate and protect the town from the landward side. Plans to level down the whole area had to be abandoned as too time-consuming.

As the bastions rose upwards from the water's edge, the rectangular grid pattern of streets, planned by Laparelli, was laid out, while a perimeter road ensured easy movement of troops and war material.

Plots were offered for sale and buildings were to conform to a high standard.

When Laparelli departed from the Island he left his Maltese assistant, Gerolamo Cassar, to continue the work he had started; this gifted architect had already made a name for himself during the Great Siege when, thanks to his expert advice, a number of Turkish siege engines were destroyed. This remarkable man was now entrusted with the building of the most important edifices of the Order in Valletta. La Valette died in 1568 and was buried in the Church of Our Lady of Victories, the first building to be erected; for the next three years he was to be the only inhabitant of the city.

The next Grand Master was hardly less enthusiastic than La Valette, and when in 1571, five years from the laying of the foundation stone, the bastions were completed, this Grand Master formally transferred the seat of the Order from Birgu across the harbour to Valletta. Other Grand Masters continued to embellish the new city and, in time, all the important buildings of the Order were enclosed within its walls: the Auberges of the Langues of the Order; the Grand Master's Palace with its Armoury; the Co-Cathedral and other churches; the Hospital; the Courts of Justice and the palatial houses of individual Knights, rich Maltese citizens, and ecclesiastics.

On a humbler tone were the buildings that housed the Mint, the Foundry and Munitions Factory, the Bakeries and the windmills for grinding the corn. In the less important streets were the houses of the artisans and other servants that were employed by the Order. Following an abortive uprising, special dungeons were built to serve as sleeping quarters for the slaves.

The Fall of the Order

When the Order made Malta its home, for the first time the masters of the Maltese lived on the Island itself, and wealth poured into the Island, rather than the other way round.

The Knights of the Order of St. John came from the noblest and richest families of Europe and a Knight was expected to pass on his property to the Order on his death, but it was not unusual for a member of the Order to make gifts and endowments during his lifetime as well.

Another source of revenue were the proceeds from captured Turkish shipping - a sort of legalized piracy, in fact.

As a result of all this, the Order was to accumulate a vast patrimony over the years, and owned many an estate in practically every country of Europe.

The Order embarked on a programme of public works that had the effect of embellishing the Island and of improving the standard of living of the islanders.

Some of the Knights were accompanied by servants who came with them from their countries of origin and these cooks, tailors and other retainers often intermarried with the islanders and, in this way, passed on their skills to them.

Many Maltese found employment with the Order as soldiers, sailors, labourers and white-collar workers. Maltese who showed talent were sent abroad under the patronage of the Order, and came back as renowned musicians, sculptors, painters and architects. Foreign artists were also encouraged to work on the Island and the result of their labours is the rich cultural heritage that the Order bequeathed to the Maltese; these artists were also responsible for the magnificent churches now being built in the villages - a fitting status-symbol of the villagers in their newly acquired wealth. Six years after the Great Siege the Turks were also defeated at sea, in the Battle of Lepanto, in which the galleys of the Order participated, but the back of the Ottoman Empire was not quite broken.

Corsair raids on Malta were less intense but the building of the Island's defences still went on unabated.

In time, however, as the Turkish Crescent waned, these attacks became less frequent and not only did Christian countries no longer require protection from the Turks, some were in fact, finding it profitable to trade with them.

In Malta people could now live outside the walled towns, and some villages that had been abandoned in the face of corsair raids were now repopulated. The country estates of the rich still had, none the less, a grim, fortress-like look about them. Some of the Maltese Nobles built themselves houses in

Valletta, but most of them preferred their ancestral palaces at Mdina, yet even these, and other buildings in the Old City, such as the seat of the Maltese elected Municipal Council (the Università), and the Cathedral itself, were rebuilt in the new Baroque style. Essential foodstuffs, particularly grain and wine, continued to be imported from Sicily, but the Knights encouraged and fostered local industries especially the cultivation and weaving of cotton. The Order kept up with the latest developments abroad, particularly in the field of Medicine: by 1769 Malta had its own University.

The Knights were also responsible for the introduction of village, and other, popular festivities most of which had a religious origin: Carnival, the festas, and, above all, the feast of Our Lady of Victories, the day the Great Siege is commemo-

rated. As the might of the Ottoman Empire weakened still further, the fleet of the Order lay idly at anchor in the Grand Harbour (the oared galleys having been replaced by round-bottomed sailing ships early in the 18th Century). The Knights, the young Knights especially, having nothing better to do, whiled away their time in activities far removed from their monastic vows. The finances of the Order were now in a precarious position. Unemployment was rife and poverty was widespread. A revolt headed by some priests was quickly crushed and the ringleaders executed or imprisoned. Towards the end of the 18th Century matters for the Order were going from bad to worse: in France, where most of her overseas property lay, the possessions of the Order were taken over by the Republican Govern-

ment and French refugees, fleeing to Malta from the Revolution, were an added drain on the treasury of the Order. In the wake of his victorious Italian campaign, Napoleon confiscated the Order's property in that country as well.

Some of the latter Grand Masters genuinely tried to rectify matters, but the rot had set in and nothing could stop it. At the time the last Grand Master of Malta, Ferdinand von Hompesch, was being elected, Napoleon was making his plans to take over the Island.

The French

Napoleon's capture of Malta in June 1798 cannot be counted as one of his military triumphs. Setting sail from Toulon on his way to conquer the East, he requested permission to enter the Grand Harbour to

water his fleet. The Grand Master, mindful of the neutral status of the Island, granted his request with the proviso that only four warships were allowed in the harbour at one time.

In expectation of such an answer, Napoleon had the invasion planned to the last detail.

A fifth column of French Knights crossed over to Napoleon as soon as he had landed and gave up the positions under their command to him.

In a short time the only places still unoccupied were the towns around the main harbours and around these the French proceeded to lay down their artillery.

The Grand Master capitulated without offering any resistence and Napoleon made his grand entry into Valletta and within a week Von Hompesch, accompanied by a few knights, left the Island unwept, unhonoured, and unsung.

Napoleon then set about introducing his reforms, not all of which were bad. Slavery was abolished and the small number of slaves then on the Island were emancipated; and even if he suppressed the University, he did introduce a primary education programme which, like the charitable institutions was to be run by the state. Napoleon's mistake in Malta was to attempt too much, too quickly. The Maltese felt that they had been let down by the Order, but before they could attempt any resistance they were talked into submission by the Bishop. Out of respect, or more likely, out of gratitude to that prelate, Napoleon gave his assurance that the rights of the Church would be safeguarded, which promise he was soon to break, however. The Bishop, on his part, issued a pastoral letter in which he reminded his flock of the teaching of St.Paul to obey the constituted authorities. Maltese who had served in the Order's army and navy were recruited into the French Republican forces, and other regiments were raised for garrison duties on the Island itself.

Nobility was, of course, abolished and all armorial bearings were to be removed - the only surviving memorials of Napoleon's occupation in Malta are a plaque on the side of Palazzo Parisio in Valletta stating that Napoleon slept there, and numerous coats-of-arms on the façade of public buildings and on bastions which, because of their position or size, could not be easily removed and for that reason were defaced by order of the French authorities.

After stripping the palaces, Auberges and other buildings of everything of value, Napoleon, conveniently forgetting his promises, next turned his attention to the churches; only such articles that were indispensable for the "exercise of the cult" were left while all other valuables were removed and priceless works of art in gold and silver melted down into ingots.

The French soon realised that promises are easier made than kept: the wives and other dependents of the sailors and soldiers that left with Napoleon for Egypt never received the pay promised to them while those who had previously been employed by the Order never got their pensions either; because Britain had the command of the sea, the export of cotton from Malta came to a standstill, this in turn, affected the farmers and many other sections of the population.

It was a young boy who started it all. History does not give us his name, all we know about him is that he was about twelve years of age. On the 2nd September 1798 the treasures of the Carmelite Church at Mdina were to be expropriated and sold by auction and a small crowd had gathered to heckle those in charge of the operation. A French commander and a sergeant ordered the crowd to disperse and it was then that the boy pelted the commander with a stone. Drawing their swords, probably with the intention of frightening the lad, the two Frenchmen were set upon and lynched on the spot by the mob.

The garrison of Mdina immediately locked the gates of the city and the Maltese, on their part, rang the church bells to raise the alarm. People from the nearby villages rushed to the Old City and, entering by way of a secret passage, quickly overpowered the soldiers.

A relieving force from Valletta was driven back with heavy losses. With the element of surprise on their side, in a matter of hours the Maltese had overrun the islands except for the fortified cities by the harbours and the two forts in Gozo. A cannon from the captured coastal forts was brought to bear on the French positions as a National Assembly was hastily convened.

Nominally the Order had held the Island of Malta in fief from the King of Sicily (since 1735 this island had been amalgamated with the State of Naples and was then known as the Kingdom of the Two Sicilies), and it was to the King of the Two Sicilies that the Maltese now turned for aid and protection. At the same time deputies were despatched to seek aid from the allies of the King, the British.

The Maltese made a plea for arms and for permission to obtain grain from Sicily on credit, the insurgents being poorly armed with only a few muskets, pikes, swords or even more simply with cudgels. A few muskets and some funds were sent by the King while British warships under Nelson, blockaded the Malta harbours to prevent aid from reaching the beleaguered French garrison.

A small number of British troops were landed and the French in Gozo surrendered in October 1798, the Sicilian flag being hoisted on the ramparts.

A plot on the part of the Maltese inside Valletta to open the gates of the city to their fellow countrymen was uncovered, and fourty-five Maltese were executed. Among those who faced the firing squad was a heroic Maltese priest - Dun Mikiel Xerri.

As the siege wore on, the French penned in the fortifications were prevented from receiving aid because of the British blockade, while the Maltese, by this time, aided by Italian and British troops, did not have the means of assaulting the formidable bastions.

The King of the Two Sicilies had been driven out of Naples by the advancing French troops and was forced to take refuge in Sicily and was in no position to proffer adequate protection to the islanders. For that reason the Maltese deputies asked permission of the King of the Two Sicilies to allow them, the Maltese, to ask for protection from His Britannic Majesty for the duration of the war. Permission was granted and Captain Ball, the captain of a British warship, was nominated president of the assembly, now renamed Congress, and under his presidency the "various and frequent dissensions of the Maltese leaders were finally pacified". Because most of the Maltese were under arms, the fields lay barren and unproductive, foodstuffs were scarce so that corn was obtained forcibly from Sicily by the British who, after this intervention, rose high in the esteem of the Maltese. The French, having arrived at the end of their tether, were ready to capitulate but the troops of Napoleon proudly refused to submit to the Maltese rebels.

The British, on the other hand, anxious to deploy their troops and warships in other theatres of war, were eager to speed up the surrender of the French in Malta.

The Maltese had borne the brunt of the fighting and other privations, but when the capitulation was being drafted and signed neither they, nor their representatives, were allowed to participate in the negotiations. The National Congress was dissolved and the Maltese Battalions disbanded; a Maltese regiment formed by the British, under British officers was, however, retained. As the British flag was hoisted in place of the French tricolour, the Maltese prepared to settle under their new masters.

The British

Once the French were expelled from the Island, the British were not so much interested in keeping Malta, as keeping the French out. In fact, at the Treaty of Amiens (1802), that brought hostilities between Britain and France to an end, it was decided that Malta was to be returned to a reformed Order of St. John under the protection of the Kingdom of the Two Sicilies and that her neutrality was to be guaranteed by all the Great Powers. The Maltese, in the majority, were thoroughly opposed to such an arrangement. If Britain refused sovereignty over the Island, it was up to the Islanders themselves to decide what was to be their fate. A mob in Valletta tore down the posters announcing the proposed return of the Knights.

However, all plans were laid aside when hostilities in Europe broke out once more, and the British gradually began to realize what the French already knew: the strategic value of the Maltese islands. Unlike their predecessors, the British retained as many institutions of the Order as was practicable, and as many Maltese as possible were installed in Government posts. Like the French before them, the British courted the Church for the powerful support it could render, and in this they were more successful than were the French.

Italian continued to be the language of culture and learning as it had been for centuries before, and official proclamations were phrased in the Italian tongue.

With the British in command of the sea, all mercantile shipping was obliged to call at the Valletta Harbour for clearance by the British Navy, and before long, the Maltese Islands became the most important centre of trade in the Mediterranean. Under the Treaty of Paris (1814) the Island was confirmed as a British Possession "... by the Voice of Europe and the Love of the Maltese" as an inscription runs.

With the cessation of hostilities, Malta lost its favoured position under the protection of the British Navy and as a plague epidemic carried away thousands, an era of wealth and prosperity for the Maltese people came to an end.

All this time the Maltese were hoping that the National Congress would be revived and that they would be able to have a say in their country's affairs; unfortunately imperial considerations took precedence, and the petitions of the Maltese upper classes fell largely on deaf ears. The Università, the Municipal Council, had been elected into office without a break from the middle of the 14th Century, but by this time its functions had been reduced to supplying the Island with grain. In 1819 this ancient institution was suppressed. Corn was now imported from Black Sea ports instead of Sicily while trade with Britain was encouraged, the intention being of severing the umbilical cord that joined Malta to Sicily. Another step in the same direction was the separation of the Bishops of Malta from the Metropolitan See of Palermo which was obtained by the British from the Pope.

As steam replaced sail, Malta became an important coaling station, all the more so after the opening of the Suez Canal in 1869. The dockyards were expanded and provided work for a sizeable section of the population. Agriculture was encouraged to make the Island Fortress as self-sufficient as possible and the growing of potatoes, now a major agricultural export, was introduced. The ever present problem of the water supply also received urgent attention.

Prosperity brought about a rapid rise in the population and emigration was actively encouraged to ease the burden on the fortress economy. Several Maltese established themselves in Egypt and in the Barbary Coast where they prospered, though some did return. Attempts to encourage Maltese to emigrate further afield, to South America and Australia, were not successful.

Italian political refugees of the Risorgimento sought refuge in Malta and the example of these Italian patriots had the effect of further fanning the flames of Maltese Nationalism.

At the insistence of the Maltese a Council of Government was set up in 1835. Composed of seven appointed members it was the first small step towards a representative government, still at this time, a long distance away.

The military worth of Malta and its islands was to be demonstrated during the Crimean War (1854-56) when the Island Fortress became a rear base for the departure of troops and a receiving station for casualties.

The building of the breakwater at the mouth of the Grand Harbour was started in 1903. It was a colossal undertaking and provided work not only for Maltese, additional labourers had to be recruited from Sicily. Once the work was completed, unhappily many Maltese found themselves out of work. Imperial policy dictated that Britain take Malta under its wing and anglicize, as far as possible, the local population. A measure of success was achieved among the working classes, they knew on which side their bread was buttered, but the upper classes retreated into their centuries-old Latin culture and gave the cold shoulder to their new masters; by so doing they were superseded by the protégés of the British. An "upstart", educated in an English university, or an English military academy, was looked down upon by an upper-class intellectual brought up and schooled in the Italian language. Before long, the Language Question, as it came to be called, lost its shibboleth value and the fight resolved itself on which of the two languages, English or Italian, were to be taught in Government schools. The Maltese tongue, the language of the people, was to receive a welcome boost from the pro-British faction which promoted the vernacular in favour of Italian as a second language.

In the meantime the question of proper representation was inching slowly towards self-determination; at times the constitution would be suspended and all reforms in this respect would then have to start from scratch.

The First World War placed Malta on a war footing and, as happened in the Crimean War sixty years earlier, Malta was to provide harbour and dockyard facilities to the Allied Navies, and her contribution in the cause of sick and wounded soldiers hospitalized on the Island earned Malta the title "Nurse of the Mediterranean".

When peace had been restored hundreds of dockyard and other workers and servicemen were

made redundant and unemployment was widespread. The price of bread soared and the discontent amongst the working classes was added to that of the higher classes who were clamouring for representation in the Island's affairs.

A National Assembly was set up to make proposals for a new constitution. During one of the public meetings of this Assembly, held on the 7th June 1919, the crowd grew hostile and the troops were called out to restore order. When the troops opened fire on the rioters, three of them were killed while another died of his wounds later. The newly appointed Governor immediately consulted the Maltese about changes in the Constitution and he did his best to mollify the population, and not long afterwards by the new Constitution, that of 1921, Malta was, at last, to be granted Self-Government with responsibility for all internal affairs. The British Government retained control on Defence; Foreign Affairs; and Immigration.

The four Maltese who died in the Sette Giugno Riots may not have died in vain.

The Path to Independence

For the Maltese People the path to independence was neither smooth nor straight.

By the time Malta was granted Self-Government in 1921 the political factions could be classified into three main groups: the pro-British group that broadly opted for the advancement of the English language and culture, as well as the dissemination of the Maltese language. The pro-Italian group stood for the use of Italian and English but also for the propagation of Italian culture; this group had within its ranks a section of the clergy who looked upon British culture as being a stepping stone to the Protestant cause and these lent their support to the more traditional, pro-Italian, party.

A newcomer to the political scene was the Labour Party, then in its infancy, its programme being com-

pulsory education, the promotion of the English and Maltese languages and, as is to be expected, the improvement of working and social conditions.

When the pro-British party in power attempted some reforms, the Church intervened and this brought down attacks from the party and counter attacks from the clergy.

In the troubles that followed elections were suspended and the Constitution was withdrawn in 1930.

In the following election the pro-Italian party with the support of the Church won at the polls with a great majority. Now that they were back in power, the Nationalist Party attempted to revive the Italian interests which had been trampled upon by the previous administration,

In the political storm that followed the Constitution was again suspended and, one year later, Malta reverted back to colonial rule. The British Government, now in sole control of the Island and unfettered by local political opinion, made Maltese and English the two official languages of the Island, which, in fact, they still are, while the use of Italian was eliminated from admin-

istrative circles. By the time the next constitution was granted World War II had started. When Italy allied herself to Germany Malta was thrown into the front line. The first attack, by Italian bombers, took place on the 11th June 1940. The first casualities during that raid were six Maltese gunners of the Royal Malta Artillery.

The extremists in the pro-Italian party were interned and exiled, and the less vociferous ones were cowed into silence. The exodus from the towns into the countryside started soon afterwards.

Using ancient catacombs and a disused railway tunnel as shelters against air-raids, other tunnels were excavated in the living rock for the same purpose. These galleries, damp and uncomfortable though they were, were instrumental in saving many lives amongst the civilian population. War in the Mediterranean theatre was predictable, yet when it did come the Island was poorly equipped to defend itself: the only fighter planes were four antiquated Gloster Gladiators. One was quickly lost and the surviving three were named "Faith, Hope and Charity" (a skeletonized Faith can be seen in the War Museum in Valletta). These planes were augmented with a few Hurricanes some weeks later. Against these, the Italian Regia Aeronautica could count on two hundred aircraft stationed in Sicily, a mere hundred kilometres from Malta. The Axis (the Germans and the Italians) were clearly anxious to occupy Malta to make sure that their supply line between Sicily and North Africa was not cut and when the Germans moved the Luftwaffe into Sicily the bombing was intensified.

As a result many buildings, especially those in the harbour area and near the airfields were flattened or badly damaged. As the Axis came to control most of North Africa as well as Greece and Crete, the supply lines to the Island from Gibraltar and Egypt were seriously threatened.

In June 1941 Hitler attacked Russia and the Luftwaffe in Sicily diverted most of its planes to that front. The air-raids on Malta eased, but did not cease entirely; at the same time, having received reinforcements, Malta took to the offensive and submarines and aircraft based on the Island attacked Axis shipping as well as ground targets in Sardinia, Sicily and even Tripoli; furthermore, by intercepting supplies from Sicily to North Africa, Rommel was deprived of many essential supplies. On 26th July 1941 the only seaborne attack, that directed against the Grand Harbour by Italian E-boats, was brave and dashing, but unsuccessful. One of the advantages of the defenders was radar, then in an early stage of development, but still a decided asset. It was radar that had alerted the Maltese gunners and foiled the E-boat attack.

When the Luftwaffe was again in Sicily in full complement the bombing commenced once more and Malta was, once again, thrown on the defensive. The airfields were under constant attack and the work of repairing the holed runways, a twenty-four hour job. Many planes were destroyed on the ground because they could not become airborne.

Munitions, fuel and other stores were running low and food was in short supply.

Throughout this ordeal, despite continuous air-raids, lack of practically all necessities, and an acute food shortage, the Maltese soldiered on. A third of the anti-aircraft crews were Maltese and they soon made a name for themselves for their bravery and efficiency.

On the 15th of April 1942 King George VI awarded the George Cross Medal to "... the brave people of the Island Fortress of Malta". A representation of this medal is now proudly displayed on the top left-hand corner of the white and red Maltese Flag. The presentation of the medal took place in the square opposite the Grand Masters' Palace in Valletta among heaps of rubble - a most appropriate backdrop for the occasion - it would have been impossible, in any case, to find an open space in the towns that was not ringed by bombed buildings.

If the morale of Malta's defenders was high, the material resources of the Island were low; with supply ships being intercepted and destroyed by Axis aircraft and submarines the situation was desperate; by July 1942 the supply of vital provisions was calculated to last two weeks. Although badly mauled, the "Santa Maria Convoy" limped into the Grand Harbour on the 15th August of that year and the situation was saved.

With replenished stores and the arrival of some hundred Spit-fires, the tables, at last, were being turned. Although Malta was still

under attack, by June 1943, it was considered sufficiently safe for King George to visit the Island to a huge welcome by the Maltese people whom he had so singularly honoured. A month later, using Malta as an advance base, the Allies invaded Sicily and the war moved away from the Island. Supplies now reached Malta regularly and the worst was over.

True to their promise made during the War, the British restored Self-Government. Fresh elections were held and the pro-Italian exiles were repatriated. With most of the inhabitants being homeless, reconstruction was the first priority of the newly elected Labour Government but social conditions were also improved.

In the dockyard area, especially, the trade union movement grew in strength as workers everywhere were becoming conscious of their rights. As happens after every war, the end of hostilities was marked by massive unemployment as servicemen and service workers were made redundant; emigration, particularly to Australia, was encouraged and organized on a vast scale. Three years later, following a split in the Labour Party, the Nationalist Party headed a Coalition Government, this party now strove to obtain a Dominion Status for the Island. The Nationalists were formerly the pro-Italian party but, since the post-war years, the image of this party was to change gradually and in the end they were even accused of being pro-British! Originally being the party of the intelligentsia, the party now attracted numerous workers within its ranks.

On the return of the Labour Party to office, a request for integration was made to the British Government with Maltese representation at Westminster. When the British cooled to the idea after evincing an initial interest the Labour Party went to the other extreme and insisted on Independence, and the Church was accused of having undermined the Integration plan by insisting that its ancient privileges be safeguarded; the acrimonies that followed were to cost the Labour Party many votes.

The Constitutional Party, the original pro-British party, died a natural death, its mission having been accomplished. In 1964 another Coalition Government, again headed by the Nationalists, was in London for an All-party Independence Conference; the Labour Party withdrew its representatives but, nevertheless, negotiations continued. In the wake of fresh elections and confirmed by a referendum, Malta achieved Independence within the Commonwealth on 21st September 1964 with the Queen of England as the nominal Queen of Malta. Under the next Labour Government, Malta was declared a Republic with Sir

Anthony Mamo as its first President. On the 31st March 1979, at the termination of the Military Base Agreement, the last British serviceman left the Island and Malta entered into its self-imposed state of neutrality. Tourism remains one of the key pillars of Malta's earnings although local manufacturing largely with foreign investors also plays an important role in the Maltese economy. The Maltese are a proud and independent people but in their heart of hearts they realise that financially Malta cannot stand alone. The Labour Party desired integration with Britain and the old-time Nationalists had yearned for integration with Italy.

By joining the European Economic Community it is possible that the Maltese people will achieve their aspirations without having to sacrifice their sovereignity in the process.

Malta has applied to join the EU and all local legislation and standards are conforming to these EU requirements.

Maltese tourism

Valletta

When Grand Master Jean Parisot de la Valette laid the foundation stone of Humilissima Civitas Vallettae the last thing that he had in mind was a city of fine palaces. Valletta was intended as a fortress to protect the two har-hours on either side of the rocky peninsula on which it was to be built.

According to tradition, the Church of Our Lady of Victories was built over the foundation stone itself. The façade of the church was altered in 1690 but is otherwise unchanged.

The first buildings to be erected were the Auberges; these were the headquarters of the different ethnic groups into which the Knights were divided. Other buildings followed until, before long, all the space was taken up by imposing palaces and churches.

Space is still at a premium in Valletta and no building is wasted: one of the Auberges is the Office of the Prime Minister, one a museum, another the General Post Office and two are Government Departments. One was demolished in 1839 to make room for the Anglican Cathedral of St. Paul. Palazzo Lanfreducci was also demolished and in its stead was built the Royal Opera House; finished in 1866 it was destroyed by enemy bombing in 1942; ever since that time the various governments have been studying plans for this site and in the meantime the bombed-out building has been partly cleared and the space used as a car park.

A block away from the ruins of the Royal Opera House is Strait Street, which was better known among sailors of the British Navy as "The Gut". Here soldiers and sailors spent their evenings in activities far removed from Grand Opera as the bars and the ladies in the Gut did a roaring trade; the only indication of its scarlet past are the fading signboards outside the establishments of the Street that is called Strait.

A number of Government Departments were obliged to move out of Valletta due to lack of space. The

University was transferred to more modern premises and the same applied to several other institutions. Most, if not all, foreign missions have also moved out of Valletta, a notable exception being the Embassy of the Sovereign Military Hospitaller Order of St. John of Jerusalem, of Rhodes and of Malta - known as the Knights of Malta. This embassy is housed in St. John's Bastion.

First recorded in 1535, the Malta Carnival became increasingly popular and is now one of the highlights of the calendar for tourists and Maltese alike. Carnival is considered to be such an important institution that the main gateway to the city, the old Porta Reale, was altered into the monstrosity it now is to permit an easier passage to the Carnival floats. On the other side of the coin, some of the older parts of Valletta have been pulled down; these relics from previous centuries were quaint and picturesque but were, at the same time, slummy and unhealthy. The new constructions, however, have been carried out tastefully and, as a rule, do not jar with the older buildings of Valletta.

The National Library, the Biblioteca, was the last building to have been built by the Order, having been finished in 1796. It houses a rich collection of books as well as medieval manuscripts and the archives of the Order. As a memento one can buy a photocopy of the deed of Emperor Charles V in which he granted Malta and its islands in fief to the Order in 1530.

For those interested in things military there is the Palace Armoury, the War Museum in Fort St. Elmo and an exact replica of the underground War Room down in Lascaris Ditch.

Even if the Opera House has yet to rise from the ashes of the Blitz (some are of the opinion that a multi-storey car park should be built there instead), music lovers and balletomanes can still go to Manoel Theatre. This gem of a building was built in 1732 and has recently been restored to its former glory for, as its builder Grand Master Anton Manoel de Vilhena would have said, "... the honest recreation of the people". For art lovers there are the Museum of Fine Arts and the Cathedral Museum.

Valletta boasts of three Parish Churches and a host of others, but pride of place must go to St. John's Co-Cathedral.

The plain exterior of this edifice grossly belies its sumptuous interior: no space is left unadorned, the walls are carved and gilt and the painted vaulted ceiling is the masterpiece, of Mattia Preti while four hundred slabs of inlaid marble pave the church. These slabs are emblazoned with the armorial bearings of the more important members of the Order.

Even a walk down the streets of Valletta can be rewarding, as long as one does not walk too fast. Many admire the magnificent Baroque façade of the Castellana, the Law Courts of the Order, few, however, notice a large iron hook let into the wall just around the corner of this building. Nobody can say for certain who put it there, or why (one theory is that it was used in hoisting the bells of St. John's Co-Cathedral across the square) but to the sailors of the British Navy this hook possessed magical powers: they believed that any sailor passing through it unaided would get a promotion. In years gone by, people, young people especially, used to troop into Valletta every evening; they filled the many cinemas there, crowded the coffee shops or just strolled up and down the main streets to admire and be admired, followed by a last-minute rush to catch the last bus to the village.

All that has now changed. The cinemas have now closed down for want of patrons and the young people drive to the latest "in" spots outside Valletta, to discotheques and country clubs leaving Valletta to brood quiely over her glorious past.

The Grand Masters' Palace

Valletta is a city of palaces but for the Maltese, the Grand Masters' Palace is known simply as il-Palazz, the Palace. The first building there was a plain wooden structure surrounded by a stone wall. The Order acquired it in 1571 but in 1572 the construction of the palace was still in its initial phase. Started by Grand Master Pietro del Monte, it fell to his successor, Jean Lesveque de la Cassière, to complete the building. Subsequent Grand Masters, whose home it was, added their improvements and embellishments; the covered wooden balconies were added as late as the middle of the 18th Century.

In its finished form the Palace is built on two floors and occupies an entire block. The two main portals, Baroque and imposing, stand in direct contrast to the unadorned treatment of the rest of the façade; three other side entrances give on to as many streets.

The Palace has all the hallmarks of its Maltese architect, Gerolamo Cassar: austere and sombre from the outside but not lacking in dignity, nonetheless.

Three of the doorways lead to a spacious courtyard while another portal and a gate lead to a smaller courtyard which is on a slightly higher level; the two courtyards are interconnected by a short flight of stairs. The larger of the two courtyards is known as Neptune's Courtyard from a bronze statue of that god. This statue was placed in its present position by the British Governor, Sir John Gaspard le Marchand who had had it removed from another part of Valletta; the visage bears a striking resemblance to that of Grand Master Alof de Wignacourt who had it set up originally.

The smaller courtyard - Prince Alfred's Courtyard is named after one of Queen Victoria's sons to commemorate his visit to Malta in 1858, but this courtyard is better known as that of Pinto's Clock. This clock has four dials showing, besides the time, the day, the month and the phases of the moon. The hours are struck by bronze effigies of Moorish slaves wielding sledge-hammers. It is said to be the work of the Maltese clockmaker Gaetano Vella and built in 1745.

Each of the two courtyards has a fountain against the walls opposite the main entrances; both are ornamental but, in their time, their function was more utilitarian than for mere show. On the walls of the cloister surrounding Neptune's Courtyard are sculptures of coats of arms that had been removed from bastions and public buildings by order of Napoleon, some of which were also defaced at the same time.

As in Renaissance palaces in Italy, the important storey was the Piano Nobile, the first floor; the ground floor being used as stables, service quarters and stores. The Main Staircase leading up to the Piano Nobile was built by Grand Master Hughes de Loubenx Verdala as advertised by the wolf in his coat of arms. This staircase has been built to the same plan as that of Verdala Palace, the imposing country retreat of the same Grand Master. Both staircases have the same shallow steps, allegedly to make it easier for knights in heavy armour to climb them. The top of the staircase gives on to a lobby formed by the angle where two of the palace corridors meet. The right-hand passage leads to what used to be the Palace Armoury but that part of the building is now the seat of the House of Representatives (the Parliamentary Assembly is composed of only one chamber, there is no Upper House) Arrangements are in hand, however, to move the House into the Auberge de Castille.

The lunettes over the windows in this passage are the work of Nicolò Nasoni da Siena and were painted in the first quarter of the 18th Century. Their opposite numbers were painted by the Maltese artist Giovanni Bonello some hundred and sixty years later; the whole set, however, is complementary and shows Maltese and Gozitan landscapes as they appeared at those times. The walls are hung with full-length portraits of various Grand Masters, one of whom, Jean Paul Lascaris Castellar, has entered the Maltese language: when a Maltese wants to describe a morose person he will say that he, or she, has Lascaris' face - wiċċ Lascri! A notable hall in the Armoury Corridor is the Council, or Tapestry, Chamber, which was the place where the members of the Order sat in Council. This chamber was also the seat of the Malta Parliament from 1921 until 1974, before the House moved to its present situation.

On being elected to that high office, a Grand Master was expected to make a gift to the Order - the Gioja. Part of the Gioja of Grand Master Ramon Perellos y Rocaful is the priceless set of Gobelins Tapestries that give the name to this chamber. Perellos was elected in 1697 but it was only in 1710 that these tapestries were completed and hung in the place for which they had been created. Les Tentures des Indes (the Indian Tapestries) is a vague title for a magnificent rendering of fauna and flora from three continents, the Noble Savage being also very much in evidence. Also in evidence are the coat of arms of the donor, the pears of Perellos woven into the tapestries themselves - with a gift of such munificence why should not the left hand know what the right hand doeth! The space between the top of the tapestry to the ceiling is taken up with scenes depicting naval battles and other activities of the Order's galleys; the different panels are divided by twelve allegorical figures representing as many Christian and Ancient Roman virtues.

Pride of place is a picture of a Cru-

The Courtyard of Neptune.

cifix to remind the Knights that they were, first and foremost, a religious order. At the time the Tapestry Chamber was being used as the House of Representatives, during one of the more heated debates, a Member threw an inkpot at the head of his opponent, unfortunately the inkpot missed its mark and hit the tapestry instead. The ink stains have been removed but after this episode MPs were only permitted the use of pencils inside the Tapestry Chamber. On one side of the door to the Tapestry Chamber is a sort of niche protected by a

grill; this niche is really the top of a well, a shaft in the thickness of the wall being connected to an ancient cistern. Tradition has it that once a year, water was drawn from this well in a silver bucket and a drink of that water was presented to a member of the noble Maltese Sciberras family by the Grand Master in person; the presentation took place inside the Tapestry Chamber as a symbolic payment by the Order as compensation to the previous owners of the land on which the Palace is built. No documentary proof of this story has come to light

- still what should an ancient well be doing on the site of a Council Chamber of the Order! To the left-hand of the lobby at the top of the Main Staircase is another corridor, known as the Entrance Corridor; this too, like the Armoury Corridor is decorated bwith paintings by Nicolò Nasini, but this time the subject chosen for the decoration of the lunettes are scenes of naval battles between the Order's galleys and those of the Ottoman Turks, apparently a subject dear to the hearts of these seafaring Knights; this passage too is lined with suits of armour and, as before, full-length portraits of Grand Masters decorate its walls. The first door to the right of the lobby leads into the State Dining Room; here the British connection is well represented by several Royal portraits: King George IV, who was Prince Regent when Britain took Malta under its wing in 1814, is portrayed, as is also Her Majesty, Queen Elizabeth II who was also Queen of Malta until the Declaration of the Republic of Malta in 1974. She is still held in high honour by the Maltese people as Head of the Commonwealth to which the Island belongs. The next door down the Entrance Corridor leads to the Hall of the Supreme Council, also known as the Throne Room. Like all the other ceilings of the Piano Nobile, the wooden ceiling of this hall is elaborately coffered and painted, but the item of greatest interest in this hall is a frieze of twelve frescoes by Matteo Perez d'Aleccio who worked in Malta between 1576 and 1581. These frescoes depict the most important events of the Great Siege and what makes them particularly interesting is that they were executed some fifteen years after that siege, and therefore well within living memory of those who had taken part in it. In the panel showing the arrival of the Piccolo Soccorso (the Little Relief), the troops are being ferried across to Birgu and, among the rowers is a brawny Maltese woman, symbolical, perhaps, of the entire Maltese population that played such an active part

Close-up of the Pinto Clock.

in that epic siege. Against the far end of the wall is the throne, occupied in turn, by the Grand Masters and the British Governors. Above the throne are now the arms of the Republic of Malta. Across the hall and opposite the throne a carved minstrels' gallery is let into the wall; this carved and painted gallery is said to have been part of the Order's flagship, the Great Carrack of Rhodes, which was one of the vessels that carried the Knights to Malta. Yet another name for the Throne Room is that of "the Hall of St. Michael and St. George" - the two warrior saints who gave their name to an order instituted by King George IV in 1818. Investure of members to that order was held in this hall, hence its name.

A door from the Throne Room leads to the Ambassadors' Room, also known as the Red Room from the colour of its damask hanging. The painted frieze shows the history of the Order before its arrival in Malta and deals mostly with the history of the Order during its long sojourn in Rhodes. In one of the panels, Knights of the Order are shown holding shields bearing the white eight-pointed (or Maltese) cross on a red background; this could be poetic licence on the part of the painter because the battle standard of the Order was a plain white cross on a red background, something like the Danish Flag; the white eight-pointed cross on a black background was more in the nature of a badge of the Order. On the walls of the Ambassadors' Room, rather appropriately, hang the portraits of a number of foreign potentates; that of the ill-fated Louis XVI carries the inscription "Donné par le Roi en l'année 1784". A door from the Ambassadors' Room leads to the Paggeria, the Pages' waiting room, also known as the Yellow Room from the gold damask covering of its walls.

Council Chamber, or Chamber of the Arrasses: Detail of the Arrasses of the Indies, made by Gobelin.

The number of the Grand Master's pages was originally eight but was later increased to sixteen. The painting of the frieze is again by Matteo Perez d'Aleccio and the subject matter is a number of episodes in the history of the Order in the Holy Land; the eight panels are divided by the inevitable allegorical figures, the one symbolising Republican Government being a strange intruder into the realm of those autocratic rulers - the Grand Masters of the Order. A door from the Pages' Waiting Room leads into a corridor which is at a right angle to the Entrance Corridor. This corridor is known as the Prince of Wales' Corridor in commemoration of a visit by King Edward VII, then Prince of Wales, in 1862. As a continuation of those in the adjoining corridor, the lunettes in the Prince of Wales' Corridor are likewise adorned with the achievements of the Order's galleys. These scenes recall the naval exploits of the Knights and add a decorative touch to the Grand Masters' Palace; but to the student of Naval History they are a mine of information since each picture carries a caption giving the date and describes the action depicted in the lunette.

The rooms giving on to this passage were formerly the private apartment of the Grand Master, afterwards they were used as the offices of the British Governors. These rooms are now the offices of the President of the Republic.

The British Governor, Sir John Gaspard le Marchand (1858-64) paved the corridors of the Piano Nobile with marble and embellished the floor with coats of arms.

Originally the sitting room of the Grand Master, one of the rooms in this wing is decorated with a frieze of frescoes illustrating the birth of the Order. On the walls of this room are portraits of various Popes: as a religious order, the Knights acknowledged the Pontiff as their supreme head and it was to the Popes that the Knights turned as the final arbiters in their internal disputes. The private chapel of the Grand Master was turned into an office for the use of the Governor's Secretary and the minstrels' gallery that was in it, removed to the Throne Room where it still is. The paintings in this chapel are probably the earliest found in the palace and show episodes from the life of St. John the Baptist, the patron saint of the Order that bears his name.

The ground floor of the palace is now taken up by various Government offices, including a number of Ministries and what were previously the palace stables now house the Palace Armoury. The armoury was transferred to this part of the palace when the original Armoury was taken over to be used as the House of Representatives. The original Palace Armoury served both as a Trophy Room and as an arsenal. Since all arms and armour of Knights of the Order, other than their swords and daggers, became the property of the Order at their death, the Armoury was always well-stocked. The finer suits of armour were carefully looked after while the less important pieces were kept in the Armoury to be used as necessary. Obsolescent arms were replaced with more modern ones from time to time; this applied particularly to firearms. The Knights frowned upon the use of firearms as being unchivalrous but they were obliged to move with the times. Registers of the arms were scrupulously kept and any taken out had to be accounted for and, at times, a refundable deposit was collected from the persons to whom they had been issued.

Unfortunately the contents of the Armoury were less well protected in subsequent periods and innumerable pieces have disappeared, some to reappear in the Louvre and in the Tower of London. Fortunately some fine specimens have been preserved, particularly the suits of armour of some of the Grand Masters. The collection, as presently displayed, is small but interesting; in

Main entrance of the upper floor, with the arms of the Republic of Malta in the foreground.

Detail of the armoury.
Page opposite: The armour of the Knights.

the old Armoury, and even more so in engravings of the Armoury as it was at one time, one is impressed by the great number of exhibits, but on the other hand, many of the specimens were repetitious, to the serious student a specimen collection is more interesting. At the time of the arrival of the Order in Malta, in 1530, the use of firearms was well on the way to revolutionizing warfare - the Great Siege was fought largely with artillery and arquebuses but armour still had its uses - a century later breastplates and shields were still being tested against firearms - in the Armoury there are several examples with dents in them to prove that they were "bulletproof". Combining the old and the new, another exhibit, is a sword incorporating a wheel-lock pistol.

St. John's Co-Cathedral

In 1573 Grand Master Jean de La Cassière authorized the construction of a conventual church of the Order of St. John. It was completed in 1578 by the Maltese architect Girolamo Cassar. Its austere exterior does not in any way betray the opulent extravagant interior. A modest portico over the main door supports the balcony used by the Grand Master to present himself to the public after election. Alessandro Algardi's bas relief of the Saviour surmounting the façade was relocated here in the 1850's from its original place in a chapel close to the entrance of the Grand Harbour. The spires on the bell towers were destroyed during the Second World War.

The rectangular Baroque interior was embellished by successive Grandmasters and further enriched by the "Gioja" or present, which every Knight was bound by statute to give on admission to the Order. Between 1662-67, Mattia Preti "Il Calabrese" painted the life of St. John the Baptist, patron saint of the Order, directly on to the primed stone of the ceiling. The Cottoner brothers paid for this work.

The walls are covered with carved gilded limestone, and the unique

pavement contains about 400 sepulchral memorials to the Order's aristocracy. These inlaid marble slabs are adorned with heraldic devices, military and naval trophies, religious motifs, and symbols befitting a necropolis.

Mazzuoli's great marble sculpture of the Baptism of Christ dominates the presbytery. The altar is made of Lapis lazuli and other rare marbles. The Episcopal throne was originally reserved for the Grand Master. The side chapels were allotted to each of the Langues of the Order.

View of the interior of the Co-Cathedral of St. John. The photograph below gives a complete view of the Flemish arrasses which are on display during the month of June.

In these chapels are buried Grand Masters belonging to that particular langue.

Zondadari's mausoleum on the left side of the main entrance is worth noting as are those of the Cottoner brothers and Perellos in the Chapel of Aragon. There is also a beautiful monument by Pradier to the Count of Beaujolais, brother of Louis Philippe of France.

The gates in the Chapel of the Holy Sacraments, like the Candlesticks on the main altar, are made of silver. These remaining treasures attest to what was perhaps the wealthiest Church of Europe before its plunder by Napoleon in 1798. In the Crypt are buried those Grand Masters who died at Malta before the Church was completed, the most important sarcophagi being those of La Valette, victor of the Great Siege of 1565 and La Cassière who built St. John's.

During the month of June a superb set of Flemish tapestries are hung in the Church. There are fourteen large and an equal number of smaller tapestries copied from paintings by Rubens, Poussin and Preti. The larger ones depict the life of Christ or symbolise the triumph of the Church. The smaller tapestries depict the Apostles. During the year these are exhibited in the adjoining Cathedral Museum which also contains relics, religious vestments and the treasure of St. John's.

In the ornate Oratory is a 3 by 5 metre painting by Caravaggio depicting the beheading of St. John.

This painting is regarded as the masterpiece of Caravaggio and is the only one of his paintings which bears his signature. The Church became a Co-Cathedral with that of Mdina in 1816.

It is without doubt one of the finest of European Churches pleasing visitors of all ages and tastes, invariably prompting Sir Walter Scott's exclamation that it was the most magnificent Church he had ever seen.

The monument to the Grand Master Manoel de Villiena.
Opposite page: Overall view of the Oratory and the splendid organ.
On p.40: The "Beheading of St. John Baptist", one of the last works of Caravaggio, situated in the Oratory.

Auberge de Provence

The Auberge de Provence was built between 1571-75 to a design by the Maltese architect Girolamo Cassar. The façade was re-designed during the first half of the 18th Century. The Auberge was the residence of the Langue de Provence, its Head, the "Gran Commandeur" being the Treasurer of the Order.

From 1824 to 1954 the building housed the British officers' Union Club, and is now the National Museum of Archeology. It contains a rich collection of prehistoric artefacts such as pottery, statuettes, stone implements, personal and other ornaments recovered from Malta's prehistoric and megalithic temple sites. Several table models of these temples are on permanent exhibition. Tomb furniture from the Punic and Roman periods is also displayed.

The Auberge de Provence:
Above: The Venus of Malta.
Opposite: Sleeping woman.
Below: One of the rooms where archaeological finds are displayed.

National Museum of Fine Arts

South Street is one of the most elegant streets in the city. It was originally known as Strada del Palazzo after the Magisterial Palace which was to be built here. This street was also known as Strada d'Albergo di Francia after the Auberge de France, destroyed during the last war, situated in it.

The National Museum of Fine Arts is one of the palaces gracing this street. This was among the first buildings erected in Valletta but it was rebuilt in its present form between 1761 and 1765. During the French occupation it was offered to the Bishop of Malta to be used as a seminary. On the capitulation of the French garrison, "Casa Miasi" as the palace then became known, was occupied by the Commander of the Anglo-Maltese troops, Captain Alexander Ball.

In 1808, Louis Charles Viscount de Beaujolais, and his brother Louis Philippe, Duke of Orléans arrived in Malta on board the French warship "Voltaire". They were lodged in this palace and it was here that the Viscount de Beaujolais died.

The premises were leased to the British naval authorities in 1821 and the palace remained the official residence of the Commander-in-Chief of the British Mediterranean Fleet. Amongst the famous admirals who occupied these premises we find Suffren de Saint Tropez, Codrington of Navarino, Fisher of Kilverstone, Keyes of Zeebrugge, Cunninghan of Hyndhope and Mountbatten of Burma.

In 1961 it was handed to the Maltese Government and in 1974 it was restored to its former glory and converted into a Museum of Fine Arts. It houses paintings, sculpture, furniture and objects connected with the Order of St. John. Permanently displayed in this Museum are works by Reni, Valentini, Stormer, Preti, Tiepolo, Favray and Perugino. A section is specially reserved for works by Maltese artists.

Temporary exhibitions and lectures are also held here.

*Valletta:
Opposite: The
Manoel
Theatre.
On this page,
above: The
Siege Bell.
Below:
Panorama of
the city.*

The War Museum, in the interior of the St. Elmo Fort.

Faith
GLOSTER GLADIATOR
THIS AEROPLANE IS THE SOLE
SURVIVOR OF THE THREE AIRCRAFT
Hone AND Charity

Auberge of Castille

The Auberge of Castille, Leon and Portugal, is the largest and perhaps finest of all the Auberges. Its head was the Grand Chancellor of the Order of St. John.

It was first built in 1574 by Girolamo Cassar on a site originally earmarked for the Magisterial Palace. Extensive reconstructions were undertaken in 1744 during Grand Master Pinto de Fonseca's term of office. Domenico Cachia, the architect responsible for these modifications was influenced by the Prefettura at Lecce and produced a very imposing façade.

Among the various monuments housed in the Upper Barrakka gardens, it is interesting to observe the bronze work "Les Gavroches" by the Maltese sculptor Antonio Sciortino (bottom right).

TO
THE RT. HONOURABLE
SIR WINSTON SPENCER CHURCHILL K

Above: Sculptural detail of the group Les Gavroches, by the Maltese sculptor, Antonio Sciortino, situated near the Upper Barrakka Gardens. Below: The statue of Queen Victoria, which stands in front of the National Library.

Lower Barrakka Gardens

At the lower end of Valletta, overlooking the entrance to the Grand Harbour are the Lower Barrakka Gardens.

The gardens afford a magnificent panoramic view, clockwise, of the Sacra Infermeria, Fort St. Elmo, the Breakwater, Fort Ricasoli, Bighi, Kalkara, Fort St. Angelo, Senglea and the Upper Barrakka Gardens. In the centre of the Gardens is an impressive Doric monument to Sir Alexander Ball who directed the blockade of the French in Valletta between 1798-1800 and later became the first British Civil Commissioner in Malta.

He died in 1809 and was buried in Fort St. Elmo. The monument was erected by public subscription in 1810 and likewise restored in 1884.

It is adorned with symbolic statues and bears an inscription round the frieze honouring Ball as the Maltese "Pater Patriae". At the base of the monument there is a Latin inscription with its English translation recording both the erection and restoration of the monument.

Our Lady of Victories Church

The Church of Our Lady of Victories was the first building to be erected in Valletta after the Great Siege of 1565. In 1617 it became the Parish Church of the Order under the care of a conventual chaplain. The façade was altered in 1690 after Grand Master Perellos placed a bust of Pope Innocent XI in recognition of the Pope's good offices in settling a dispute between Bishop Palmieri and the Prior of the Order. (Photo above)

The paintings in the ceiling, are by the Maltese artist Alessio Erardi. Inside the church is a marble bust to the Venetian Admiral Angelo Eno (1732-92) who died in Malta shortly after his victorious Tunisian Campaign.

The Vittoria, as it is known, ceased to be a Parish Church on the expulsion of the Knights of St. John from the island.

Msida, Sliema and St. Julians

Around the 1850s Sliema became a summer resort for the well-to-do and, before long, the resort grew into a town. The rich built their villas on the ridge, away from the slummy end where the fisher folk lived. As the British servicemen left, the tourists moved in, and the houses of Sliema: the villas and the hovels, were pulled down and blocks of flats and hotels rose up in their stead. A fort built by the British in 1872 is now an excellent pizzeria.

The promenade is probably the most densely populated area in the Island as strollers enjoy the sea-breezes in the cool of the summer evenings. St. Julians, its suburb, can claim an older ancestry. Originally

Above: The tourist port of Msida.
Below: The "Fortizza".

this hamlet sprang up around the old chapel dedicated to Saint Julian, patron of huting (first built in 1580, but many times rebuilt). The hunting lodges of the Knights have all disappeared except for that of Bali' Spinola who gave his name to the environs of the fishing harbour of St. Julians. Where the old hunting lodges once were are now the large number of hotels, restaurants and pubs that make of St. Julians the most bustling and popular tourist resort in Malta, especially with the younger set.

Above: The Mount Carmel Church.
Below: The little harbour of Spinola.

Msida: The Parish Church.

The Three Cities

Collectively known as the Three Cities, individually, the towns by the harbour are known by several names; however, Birgu, Bormla and Senglea are the names by which they are most commonly known.

In the beginning there was Birgu, then a small fishing village sheltering behind a castle of unknown antiquity that stood at the very tip of the peninsula. The castle, as the Castrum Maris, or Castell 'a Mare, is mentioned in several medieval documents. Apparently the Castellan had a measure of autonomy and was independent of the Università, the municipal council with its seat at Mdina, and it also appears that the people whose houses were outside the wall of this castle considered themselves as being under the jurisdiction of the Castellan and beyond that of the Università which led to much bad blood between the two bodies.

On their arrival in 1530 the Knights decided to settle in Birgu as Mdina was too far inland, and immediately set about protecting that hamlet with bastions. Castell 'a Mare was strengthened and separated from Birgu by a ditch. Not long afterwards, the adjacent peninsula, then uninhabited and known as l'Isla was likewise protected by bastions and by the time Claude de la Sengle was Grand Master it was sufficiently inhabited to merit the name of "Città Senglea" named, of course, after the Grand Master.

During the Great Siege of 1565 the inhabitants of Birgu and Senglea showed such outstanding courage that the two towns received the honorific titles of Città Vittoriosa (the Victorious City), and Città Invitta (the Unconquered City) respectively.

The conurbation that linked Birgu and Senglea was named "Bormla" and as successive Grand Masters enclosed all three cities with imposing lines of bastions, Bormla received the title of Città Cospicua (the Noteworthy). As Valletta was being built, the Knights transferred their seat of government from Birgu to that town but the three cities were still very much the centre of the naval activities of the Order; here were the shipyards and the arsenals, and here lived the Maltese seamen and ship chandlers.

Piracy was a profession of long standing, but with the arrival of the Order, Maltese corsairs achieved respectability by operating under licence from the Grand Master; and by being taxed on their booty!

Merchants of several nationalities lived in the Three Cities and traded in slaves and other merchandise acquired by the corsairs and galleys of the Order. The cosmopolitan character of the Three Cities is still discernible: there are more "foreign" Maltese surnames in this part of the Island than in any other.

Under the British, the Three Cities were a hive of activity as the Grand Harbour became the home base of the British Mediterranean Fleet, and at the same time several rich Maltese shipowning families settled in Birgu and Senglea. The docks were enlarged and increased in number and the Castell 'a Mare, which the Knights had renamed Sant Angelo, now became a shore establishment of the Navy under the name of H.M.S. St. Angelo.

Being in close proximity to military installations, the Three Cities suffered terribly as a result of enemy bombing, Senglea in particular.

View of the Sant'Angelo Fort in Vittoriosa and St. Michael's Fort in Senglea.

The inhabitants were evacuated to the relative safety of the countryside but many a historic building was irreparably destroyed.

With the granting of Independence and the subsequent closing down of the military base (a tableau in bronze recreates the farewell ceremony), oil tankers and freighters have replaced destroyers and cruisers in the dockyards.

Birgu, despite the Blitz, still has a lot to offer the visitor, such as a number of 16th Century houses in which the Knights made their abode on their arrival; the Inquisitor's Palace which incorporates a Folk Museum; and the magnificent Church of St. Lawrence.

For the more active, a walk around the bastions of Senglea with a camera can be rewarding.

Church of St. Lawrence in Birgu.
Below: Valletta seen from Senglea.

View of Vittoriosa.

The Maritime
Museum.

The Hypogeum

Hypogeum is derived from the Greek hypógeios, meaning underground, a convenient, non-committal, name for an extraordinary set of mysterious underground chambers connected by passages and steps dating to around 2,400BC. According to one theory, the complex had its beginnings as a natural cave at the back of a temple; using only flint tools, this cave was progressively enlarged and embellished by being carved in exact imitation of a built temple. An intriguing part of the Hypogeum is what is known as the "Oracle Chamber" which was probably accessible only to the initiated; inside this chamber is a shallow hole in the wall, something like a niche. The voice of a man facing it will echo eerily but the higher-pitched female voice has no such effect.

Assuming that the Hypogeum was, indeed, used as a temple, at one time it was used as an ossuary instead (some are of the opinion that the two functions were contemporary). The fragmented remains of some 7,000 skeletons, previously buried elsewhere and later deposited here, were found mixed with ochre.

It is possible that the temple ceremonies had some relationship with the cult of the dead, or even ancestor worship, but this cannot be proved though it is not inconceivable that the two were closely interconnected.

Tarxien Temples

In no other site in Malta is the evolution of prehistoric temple building better exemplified than it is at the megalithic temples of Tarxien. The earliest temple, now unfortunately in a vestigial state, goes back to around 2,800BC while the more recent of the four temples burst out in a blaze of splendour some seven hundred years later. The spiral, as a decorative motif, is found in many places in Europe from the North Atlantic seaboard to the Aegean; the ones at Tarxien, however, might have been invented, or at least developed, independently. Inside these temples has been found what, for that age, was the most colossal stone sculpture then in existence: originally 2.50 metres in height, the statue, presumably representing a Mother Goddess, has been broken in half and the top part is missing. There is a lot of conjecture about the significance of the Fat Lady statues found in most of the Maltese temples, it is possible that they are examples of female fertility deities prevalent throughout the lands bordering the Mediterranean.

Around 1,800BC the temples, having been abandoned for about two hundred years, were reused by Bronze Age folk as crematoria and as repositories of the ashes of their dead.

Żabbar Church

The building of the Church of Our Lady of Graces was started in 1641 at the instigation of the Parish Priest Don Francesco Piscopo and was completed in 1660 according to one version, and in 1696 according to another. A Maltese proverb says "a church is never finished", which is another way of stating that the people in a particular parish are never satisfied with their own church and, depending on their means, are forever improving it, the moving spirit being the ambition that the church in one's village be better and bigger than the church in the next parish. The good people of Żabbar are no exception.

Largely from the private funds of the Parish Priest Andrea Buhagiar in addition to money collected from the people of Żabbar, work on embellishing the church was started in 1738.

The Maltese architect Giovanni Bonavia redesigned the façade and two belltowers were erected; in addition the church was paved in marble and provided with a crypt.

The main painting of the Madonna and Child is a work by the painter Alessio Erardi (1669-1727).

Marsaxlokk

Marsaxlokk, the harbour to the south-east, is now a small but picturesque harbour where the brightly coloured fishing boats ride at anchor and where the wives of the fishermen knot nylon string bags for the tourists. But Marsaxlokk is also a microcosm of the historical past of the Island. A short distance from this village is the archeological site of Tas-Silg, still in the process of being excavated; at this place are the remains of Late Neolithic megalithic buildings much disturbed by superimposed Punic and Byzantine structures; here too are the only remains of a mosque to be found on the Island. Norman coins have also been found at Tas-Silg. To oppose the landing of corsairs in that harbour a fort was erected at its entrance by the Order, that of San Lucian; used as a munitions depot during World War II, it now houses the Marine Research Centre. Marsaxlokk Bay, of which the fishing harbour of Marsaxlokk forms part, is now being converted into a port for container ships.

Għar Dalam

At the time the Maltese islands were an extension of the Italian mainland, animals like elephant, hippos, deer and foxes roamed the land. With the rising of the sea-level, or the sinking of the land, or both, the islands were separated from the land mass and these animals were marooned. This took place in the Quaternary Era, some 10,000 years ago, and not during the Pliocene, eleven million to one million years ago, as was once thought to have been the case.

In time these stranded animals gradually evolved into an island sub-race resulting in a degeneration in some of the species. Fossil bones of animals have been discovered in caves and fissures in various parts of the island, but the largest concentration to be discovered so far is that at Għar Dalam.

In 1917 two human molars were found in this cave and believed, at the time of their discovery, to be those of Neanderthal Man. However, these molars have now been assigned to a much later period and it can be assumed that when the animals died, and their bones carried into Għar Dalam by the action of flowing water, Man had not yet arrived in Malta. Stone Age Man did use Għar Dalam as his abode around 4,000BC but, by this time these animals had become extinct in the Maltese Islands.

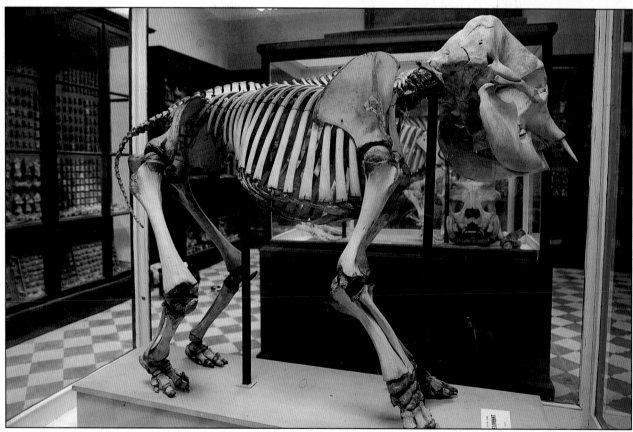

Wied iż-Żurrieq and the Blue Grotto

The western coast of Malta is steep and precipitous but in places gaps in the cliffs slope down to sea-level. One such gap is Wied iż-Żurrieq. Looking like a miniature fjord, this narrow arm of the sea is an anchorage for boats in calm weather; at the first sign of a storm the boats are winched up a steep slipway and landed.

The boats at Wied iż-Żurrieq were, and still are, used for fishing; now, however, the fishermen are finding out that it is more lucrative to take visitors to the nearby Blue Grotto.

The presence of this deep sea-cave in which the sea bottom is of an unbelievably intense blue has long been known to the fisher folk; in fact; during World War II, when an air-raid alarm was sounded, the people here took to their boats and rowed into the cave for safety.

The Blue Grotto.

The fishermen of the village Wied iż-Żurrieq run boat trips to visit the fascinating Blue Grotto.

Ħaġar Qim

This Copper Age temple was originally built about 2,700 BC but during the same period it underwent several modifications. For some unknown reason the axis of the first temple was altered and the temple itself was several times extended.

The kind of stone used in the building of this temple (Globigerina Limestone) is rather soft and relatively simple to work; possibly for this reason there are several "porthole" openings in Ħaġar Qim.

A monolith on the outside of the temple wall has been tentatively interpreted as evidence of phallic worship. A pillar "altar" with an unusual palm frond decorative carving has been found in this temple, but not in any other; it is possible that this pillar was not originally part of the temple furniture and was placed there at a later date.

Mnajdra

Perhaps having learned that Glo-bigerina Limestone does not resist bad weather the builders of Mnajdra constructed this temple out of the harder Coralline Limestone which, however, was difficult to work, while the interior walls were faced with a softer kind of limestone.

The best preserved of the three Mnajdra temples is interesting for the secret chambers that are hidden inside the thickness of its walls; these chambers communicate with the temple proper by holes bored through the wall; it is surmised that statues of gods, or goddesses, could have been placed in front of these holes and the "priest" hiding in the oracle chamber was the voice of the deity as this "spoke" to the faithful. A healing cult could have been practised in this temple because a number of baked-clay models of parts of the human body, showing symptoms of disease, have been found here.

Ta' Qali Crafts Village

The military airstrip had been abandoned for many years when somebody started using the disused hangar as a workshop for glass-blowing. And so it came about that the Ta' Qali Crafts Village was born.

In a short time the Nissen huts there were taken over by other craftsmen and new huts built. Traditional arts like pottery, silver and gold filigree, and lace making were collected in one place soon to be joined by other, possibly less traditional, handicrafts.

Among the light industries carried on at Ta' Qali is the making of polished stone ornaments using Malta "marble" as raw material; the Malta Stone workshop carries a sign offering the visitor a "piece of Malta" to take back home. For those who want to take back a piece of Maltese history one can buy a replica of a knight's suit of armour (they come in all sizes) or even a pottery copy of the Fat Lady.

The valuable blown glass made by the skilled craftmen of Mdina Glass at Ta' Qali.

Mosta

Mosta is roughly in the geographical center of the Island of Malta and, in times gone by, it was considered to be far enough inland to be relatively safe from corsair attacks. The chief attraction is now the monumental church whose design was inspired by the Pantheon in Rome. Its dome is the fourth largest in Europe: the three other domes being in Rome, London, and Xewkija in Gozo. The building was started in 1833 and the church was consecrated in 1871; it was built around and over an older church which continued to be used during the time work was in progress. In the machine age in which we are living this sounds like an exceedingly long time, but one should bear in mind that the labour on this church was done on a voluntary basis, in the little spare time the people had at their disposal. This church, like many other of the older churches in Malta, could be said to be a monument of faith. In 1942 a thousand pound bomb penetrated the dome but failed to explode.

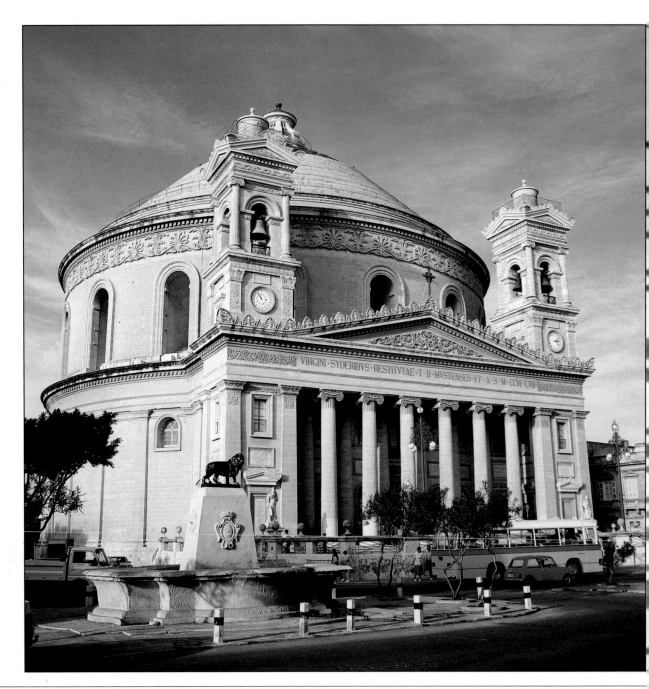

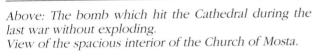

Above: The bomb which hit the Cathedral during the last war without exploding.
View of the spacious interior of the Church of Mosta.

Buġibba

Until a few short years ago Buġibba and its extension Qawra were a rocky and barren headland, yet not without its points of interest; at its tip is a small coastal battery of the Order which surrounds an older watchtower. Further inland is a small prehistoric temple, in a poor state of preservation, this temple is unique in that it was decorated with carvings of fish (these bas-reliefs are now preserved in the National Museum of Archeology in Valletta).

Buġibba and Qawra are now one of the most popular summer resorts to the north of the Island: with all the noise and bustle so beloved by holiday-makers who like that kind of "rest".

The tower and battery at the tip of Qawra has now been turned into a restaurant while the prehistoric temple is now preserved in situ within the precincts of a hotel.

St. Paul's Bay

St. Paul's Bay is one of the older seaside resorts. At the turn of the century it was the fashion for persons of means to have a second home on the coast in which to pass the hot summer months in peace and quiet but also in comfort. St. Paul's is now a residential area but an aura of tranquility still pervades the place.

The town of San Pawl il-Bahar (more accurately translated as St. Paul by-the-sea, rather than St. Paul's Bay) has many reminders of its namesake - the Apostle of the Gentiles. Here one can see Għajn Rażul, the Apostle's Fount, at which the saint is reputed to have quenched his thirst following his shipwreck; the church at tal-Ħuġġieġa, the church of the bonfire, marking the site where the apostle shook off the viper into the flames and the church at San Pawl Milqgħi, the place where St. Paul was made welcome by Publius, the Roman Governor. A number of churches have been built in succession on this last site and, significantly, in the lowest level of the dig, Roman remains have come to light.

Mellieħa

In the old maps, two landmarks are indicated to the north of the Maltese Islands: the saltpans, and the old church of Mellieħa. The production of salt has been moved to another place (the old saltpans were once sited where the Ghadira Bird Sanctuary now stands), but the old semi-underground church dedicated to Our Lady still stands; in it a fresco of the Virgin Mary was, according to tradition, been painted by St. Luke himself who, with St. Paul, was shipwrecked not far from here in the year 60. Scientific study of the icon has assigned it to a more recent, but still very ancient period.

The old saltpans are gone but they have given their name to the town of Mellieħa, melh being the Maltese word for "salt".

Most of the sandy beaches, none of them very big, are found to the north of Malta, not far from Mellieħa, the largest being at Mellieħa Bay itself.

View of Mellieħa and the Tower of Selmun.

Comino

For long periods of its history Comino was an unsafe place in which to live, nevertheless, people did inhabit this tiny island on and off, the population figures fluctuating from nil to sparse.

In 1416 the Maltese petitioned the Aragonese king, Alphonse V, to build a tower on Comino as a deterrent to the corsairs who made it their base, but the people of the Island had to wait two hundred years before work was taken in hand; eventually the Tower of Comino was finished under Grand Master Alof de Wignacourt in 1618. Despite the protection of the tower, people were chary of making Comino their home; in fact, the ancient church here, was desecrated in 1667 as being derelict; in 1716 the church was repaired and reconsecrated and, by this time the island had been repopulated to some extent. With its handful of resident families and a single hotel, Comino, even now, has an air of a forsaken but beautiful island.

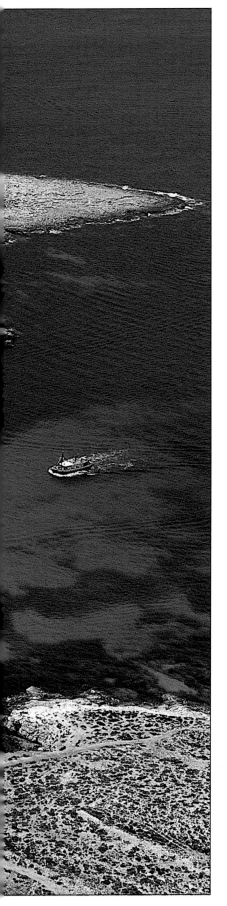

Gozo

Some years ago it was planned to connect the islands of Malta and Gozo by a bridge and Japanese engineers were called in to carry out a feasibility study. The project was considered technically possible but as the expense involved would have been considerable the plan was shelved. And many people in Malta, and many more in Gozo breathed a sigh of relief.

Should the Island of Gozo become too accessible there is a real danger of the island losing the old-word charm which Gozo has so far retained, and which Malta possessed and, unfortunately, lost some half century ago. The sister island of Malta is different from the larger island in that it is more fertile, more picturesque, and far more unspoilt; but what makes Gozo so markedly different from Malta are the Gozitans.

These frugal and tough people seem to be proof against any adversity, their character, like steel, has been tempered in the fire of privations and constant danger and they, and their descendants, have come out as better men from their ordeal.

Malta and Gozo share the same history and historical remains are duplicated in both islands, but Gozo has had more than its share of misfortunes. Largely undefended, the island was many times devastated by piratical attacks and on one occasion almost the whole of the population was carried away into slavery. When the Gozitans had advance warning of an impending invasion, such as that of the Great Siege, some of them sought refuge in the better fortified towns of Malta and some of the old people were evacuated to Sicily, but as soon as it was safe for them to do so, they always returned home; Gozitans ransomed from slavery also returned home, it never entered their minds to settle in a safer place; Gozitan emigrants who strike it rich in the countries of their adoption likewise return home and build showy houses for themselves as evidence of their success. Perhaps what makes Gozo what it is, is the love and quiet pride of its inhabitants for their homeland. This pride

Above: aerial view of the Citadel.

The little port of Mgarr, together with the new port. It has always been Gozo's only link with the outside world.

is reflected, among other things, in the size and beauty of their churches. The love which the Gozitans have for their island is also infectious: many a casual visitor has been enchanted by the island and decided to make it his home and ended by becoming himself a Gozitan (a notable exception being Ulysses who, after a stay of seven years managed to escape from the embraces of the nymph Calypso, who is supposed to have lived in Gozo). Rustic, and living in the past, Gozo may be, but that does not make the Gozitans in any way backward: opera stars of international repute are invited to sing in the two theatres in Gozo's capital, Victoria (renamed from "Rabat" in honour of Queen Victoria). For the younger generation, pop singers and music festivals provide the more modern equivalent. Moreover, some of the best brains in Malta have come out of Gozo. Like rustic communities elsewhere, but especially where economic conditions are hard, Gozitans are thrifty, but their husbandry never encroaches on avarice, and their generosity towards worthy causes is always unstinted. Until a friendship is established, a Gozitan might be reticent, but once you make a Gozitan friend, you will have made a friend for life. The citadel in Victoria is a museum in itself; it is here that the rich Medieval families of Gozo had their own quarters in which to spend the night. In the esplanade below, in the square known as It-Tokk, one can see the more colourful side of Gozo. In the open market and in the souvenir shops around it are exposed for sale such local handicrafts as crocheted woollen dresses, the wool spun from the local sheep and the dresses worked by the island's women, as is also the famous Gozo Lace, a traditional, but still a very much flourishing, art. Even if the Malta-Gozo bridge has not been built, communication between the islands is easy and frequent as car-ferries, hovercraft and yachts crisscross the six kilometre wide Gozo Channel. May the increasing hordes of visitors to that island not spoil its character and turn it into a smaller Malta.

The Citadel is built on the summit of one of the many high plateaux in Gozo.
Opposite: The Cathedral designed by the Maltese architect Lorenzo Gafa, in the form of a Latin cross. It was built over the exact site of the previous church.

The interior of the Cathedral. Opposite: the Parish Church of St. George.

Folklore Museum

This Museum is housed in three late medieval houses with Sicilian influenced architectural features. Exhibits consist of agricultural implements which include a mill for grinding corn, items related to the cotton industry, tools used in different crafts and some traditional costumes.

Archaeological Museum

All archaeological material found in Gozo is now shown in this 17th century house known as Casa Bondi. Of special interest are sherds of the Ghar Dalam phase (5000 B.C.) found at Ghajn Abdul, probably the oldest ever found in the Maltese islands and the Majmuna tombstone, a beautiful marble inscription in Kufic characters dating to 1174 A.D.

The Folklore Museum: ancient grinding machine for corn.

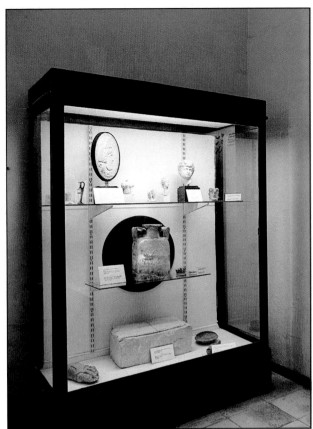

The Archaeological Museum: In the Museum many finds are on display from excavations carried out on the island, or from ancient ships wrecked along the coast.

Xlendi

This is another summer resort used by the locals and tourists alike. In 1961 two shipwrecks dating to about the 2nd century B.C. and 5th A.D. were located on the sea-bed at the mouth of Xlendi Creek under 35 metres of water. Many amphorae and several lead anchor stocks have been recovered from these wrecks and are now in the Gozo Museum of Archaeology.

Dwejra

Dwejra is an area of outstanding natural beauty on the north-western coast of Gozo. It has been an attraction to the visitor for many centuries and we have representations of the Fungus Rock on many old engravings. The area in itself is a museum of history, archaeology, natural history and geology.

Ta' Pinu Sanctuary

This is a national shrine and a centre of pilgrimages for both the Gozitans and the Maltese. The present church was started in 1920 and consecrated in 1931. It was raised to the dignity of Basilica by Pope Pius IX a year later.

The Zerka Window.
This is a massive natural archway cropping out of the sea.

The mushroom-shaped rock, locally known as the "General's Rock".

NINU'S GROTTO.

Ninu's Cave is situated at No. 17 January Str., Xaghra, near the church.

In this grotto one can see multitudes of stalactites hanging like icicles from the ceiling while many different formations of stalagmites crop up from the floor of the cave.

CALYPSO'S CAVE.

Calypso's Cave takes one back to the legendary days of Homer. Though it is hard to compare the present state of the cave and its surroundings with Homer's description of Calypso's dwelling place, prehistoric sherds of the Ġgantija phase, 3600 B.C., have been found a few metres away from the mouth of the cave.

Ġgantija Temples

The Ġgantija or, as it was commonly known in the past, "The Giants' Tower", is the best preserved and by far the most impressive prehistoric temple. It is probably the finest of all ancient remains in these islands comparing with Stonehenge for grandeur. It was cleared round about 1826.

Though no records survive of this operation, the most important find during this dig were the two stone heads of statuettes, now preserved in the Gozo Museum of Archaeology.

Ġgantija consists of two separate systems of courtyards which, like the Mnajdra Temples, do not interconnect. They are known as the South Temple which is bigger, earlier (c. 3600 B.C.) and better preserved, incorporating five large apses and the North Temple which is smaller and a later addition (c. 3000 B.C.) in a 4-apse form. The great court of the South Temple measures 23 metres from apse to apse and the height of the wall here is preserved to eight metres, the highest in all the temples. Here one notices how the successive courses of stone draw on the manner of corbelling, though it is not possible that the aperture at the top was roofed with stones. The arch was not yet known in building construction and the span of the apses here is quite large for any conceivable stone roofing. Wood or hides might originally have been used as roofing material.

Two kinds of stone were used in the construction; "talfranka", the soft stone mainly used inside as portals and floor slabs, and "talqawwi", the hard stone which is mostly used for the general construction of the walls. The interior of the walls was plastered and painted with red ochre. Traces of this have been found. The huge megaliths, forming the outer wall (the largest weighing several tons) were built alternately, one horizontally and one upright. The space between the inner and outer walls is filled with rubble and earth. It is such a system which has given the Ġgantija the stability to withstand the depredations of over 5000 years. The floor is partly covered with soft stone slabs and partly with "torba", or beaten earth. Spiral and pitted designs decorate some

of the soft stone slabs. One can hardly see the spirals today but considering their good state of preservation when the site was uncovered, this indicates that the temples had some kind of roofing protection during their use.

Għajn Tuffieħa

In Malta one cannot escape from history. When one goes for a swim, no matter where, one is always under the watchful eye of one of the coastal towers. These square two-storied towers are known as the "de Redin" towers because most of them (but not all) were built by Grand Master Martin de Redin during the middle of the 17th Century.

A cannon was fired by day and a beacon lit at night, and on the alarm being given, the towers to the left and to the right repeated the signal and within a short time the whole coastline was alerted in this way.

The Għajn Tuffieħa Tower overlooks two sandy beaches; one of the bays, the larger one, has had its name changed from il-Ramla Mixquqa (the Beach of Cracks, from the fissured cliffs surrounding it), to Military Bay when it was out of bounds as being in the Għajn Tuffieħa Camp (part of the old barracks has been converted into a holiday complex), and finally to the name it now bears: "Golden Bay".

Here is a piece of Malta that has, thankfully, been spared; except for a change of name and the intrusion of a hotel, the scene must have changed little from the time when men on the watchtower peered anxiously towards the horizon for a sign of an enemy sail.

Rabat and Mdina

The Rabat plateau is ideally suited for the building of a settlement, being, as it is, sited almost in the center of the island as well as being on high ground that could be easily defended. Man must have realized this soon after his arrival in Malta. Once it was inhabited the area has continued to be lived in ever since, generation after generation, and as one overlord replaced another.

What is certain is that the Romans built their principal city here and named it Melita, which was also the name they gave to the largest island in the archipelago (200BC). In all likelihood the Phoenicians were established here before them; in fact, Phoenician remains were found in the neighbourhood as well as later Punic-Roman remains. It is possible that the Phoenicians were not the first people to have occupied the Rabat plateau either, but any remains of an earlier period would be buried deep under the foundations of other, more recent, buildings. The next people to have lived in this part of the island were the Arabs (870AD), who separated about a third of the Roman town of Melita and surrounded it by ramparts and a ditch. They also cleared a space outside this citadel, a sort of no-man's-land, to make the citadel more secure from attack. The citadel they named Mdina (the Town) and the rest of the old settlement they named Rabat (the Suburb), the names by which they are still known. During the Medieval period Mdina was the seat of the Municipal government and an administrative center as well as a mustering station for the militia at the approach of the enemy, while, at the same time, the people from the surrounding countryside took refuge inside its walls.

Perhaps the people living in this area which was, and still is, among the most fertile and well-watered in Malta, felt safe from sudden attack and lived their own lives in small hamlets scattered around Rabat and only went into Mdina for refuge or for reasons of trade.

At this time too, a number of Religious Orders built their monasteries outside the walls of Mdina and established themselves at Rabat and its surroundings. Grim and fortress-like when they were first built, these monasteries are now surrounded by modern buildings and some of them have been modernized beyond recognition.

With the coming of the Order (1530), the Knights found out they would be better served if they established themselves by the harbour where their galleys lay at anchor, and by so doing, they left Mdina and its inhabitants undisturbed. When Valletta was built and eventually became the capital of the Maltese Islands in 1571, Mdina was relegated to that of Città Vecchia (the Old City). Some of the inhabitants of Mdina did migrate to the new city but among those who stayed on were the aristocratic families of Malta who still occupied their ancestral homes there; this had the fortunate effect of preserving a number of old 14th and 15th Century houses and palaces. The ones that had been rebuilt in the, then new, Baroque style were a number that had been demolished by the earthquake of 1693; among these is the magnificent cathedral dedicated to the Conversion of Saint Paul. The old Maltese aristocratic families owned vast rural property and from time immemorial the farmers came to Mdina to pay their yearly dues to these nobles on the traditional date of the Mnarja (an ancient harvest festival, Christianized into the feast of Saints Peter and Paul). This feast was, and still is, celebrated under the trees of Malta's nearest thing to a forest, the Buskett. In this place the Grand Masters built a hunting lodge and summer retreat in 1586 known as Verdala Castle. Horse and donkey races are still part of the Mnarja cel-ebrations. Because Roman Law forbade burials inside the city, the catacombs were located outside the walls of Melita and here too, according to tradition, is the cave in which St. Paul was kept prisoner for three months. These sets of catacombs, together with the churches built in their proximity are now Rabat's chief tourist attraction.

In Rabat one can still come across old bars bearing such names as the Windsor Castle, the Silver Jubilee (of Queen Victoria) etc. These and many others, now gone, once catered for the British soldiers stationed in the nearby Mtarfa Barracks and Military Hospital, formerly the Roman Temple of Proserpine, and now a housing estate and old people's home respectively.

Rabat - Museum of Roman Antiquities

The misnamed Roman "villa" Museum covers the site of a rich and sumptuously decorated town house belonging to a wealthy person in Roman Malta. The site, discovered in 1881 and further excavated in 1920-24, contains a number of remarkably fine mosaic polychrome pavements and some original architectural elements. A number of rooms were constructed to protect the mosaics and an upper hall was added to provide exhibition space and a suitable entrance. The porticoed neo-classical façade was completed in 1925. The main attraction are the mosaics, rated among the finest and oldest from the West Mediterranean and compare with those of Sicily and Pompeii. Originally these mosaics paved the peristyle, once support-

ed by 16 columns and two adjacent rooms. One of the pavements has only survived poorly in patches; the other rooms are characterized by an illusion of three dimensional depth.

St. Paul's Collegiate Church

St Paul's Collegiate Church is constructed upon, but to the left of St Paul's Grotto, just outside the walls and in the ditch of the old city, hence its mention in old documents as St Paul outside The Walls. The earliest documentary evidence referring to it dates from 1372. A Mediaeval cemetery with many private chapels and memorials flourished on the left of the Church.

The dedication to St Paul is due to the immemorial tradition of St Paul's use of the cave as a base for his preaching and building of an incipient Christian community during his three month stay in Malta in A.D. 60. For this reason St Paul's Grotto was described by the Cathedral Chapter as "the foundation stone of the Church in Malta". Grand Master Alof de Wignacourt soon transformed it into a Collegiate of the Order, constructed a college of chaplains officiating the new Institution and erected a Collegio as well as a new church of St Publius, adjacent to St Paul's Parish Church. The Order of St John enriched the place with various works of art, including a fine altarpiece of St Publius by Mattia Preti, an altarpiece of the Eucharist by Francesco Zahra (1710-1773), a statue of St Paul over his altar in the Grotto executed by the Maltese sculptor Melchiorre Gafa' though completed by his master Ercole Ferrata, following Gafa's, death, precious silverplate and a fine 18th cent. Neapolitan organ by Giuseppe del Piano.

The Collegiate Church of St. Paul.

Museum of St Paul's Church. The Collegio (Wignacourt College) was converted to a Museum in 1981. The access is either from the main door or else from an underground passage hewn in the rock in 1683 and linking the former residence of the officiating clergy with their church. Below, on the left, St Jerome, a Bohemian school work and on the right Grand Master Francisco Ximenez Detexada are on display in the Chapter Hall.

The Grotto of St. Paul.

Below: The Museum of the Church of St. Paul - the "College" was trasformed into a Museum in 1981.

The Crypt of St. Agatha, where the very fine frescos attributed to Salvatore d'Antonio can be found.

Mdina

On the side: the Main Gate to the City was erected in 1724 by Grand Master De Vilhena, replacing an earlier draw-bridge gate the outline of which, now walled up, is still visible some metres away to the right of the present gate. It is reached by a narrow stone bridge, over a moat dug out by the Arabs, and decorated with stone trophies of arms supported by Lions - the lion forms part of Grand Master Vilhena's escutcheon.

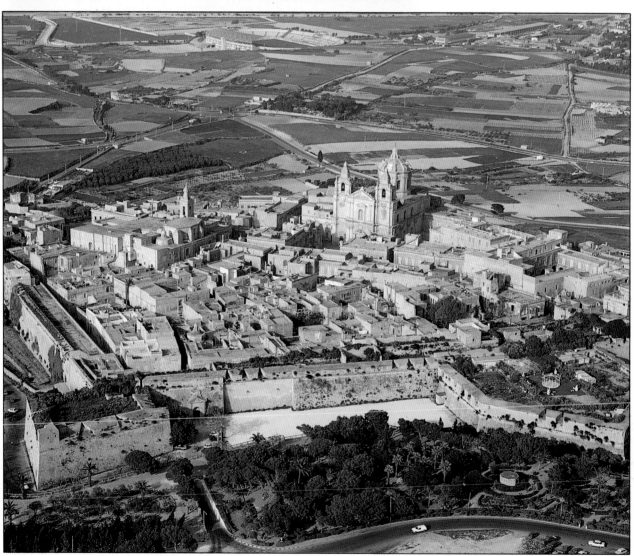

Cathedral Museum

The Cathedral Museum in Archbishop Square is an imposing baroque palace housing rich collections of art and archaeology as well as important archives. The building, completed in 1744, was constructed as a Diocesan Seminary and served its purpose up to the first decade of the present century; it was then utilized by various ecclesiastical and educational institutions until on 5 January 1969 it was inaugurated by Sir Maurice Dorman, Governor-General of Malta, as the Cathedral's Museum. The main bulk of the art collections is a legacy by Count Saverio Marchese 1757-1833).

A newly opened large room on the right of the entrance serves for the temporary display of new acquisitions but the room is also offered to local artists for exhibiting their latest works and holding one-man exhibitions.

A panel of the ancient Umbrian School, depicting St. Catherine of Siena.
Below: The Expulsion from Eden, by Bernardo Strozzi.
Opposite: The masterpiece of the Museum's picture gallery is the polyptych of St. Paul which until 1682 was the altarpiece of the former Cathedral. Subsequently it was replaced by a painting by Mattia Preti; however, the central part was preserved and placed beneath its successor.

Cathedral Church

According to tradition Malta's earliest Cathedral was dedicated to the Blessed Virgin, Mother of God, dilapidated in the Muslim period and reconstructed and re-dedicated to St Paul after the Norman conquest.

This old church was modified and enlarged several times. In 1419 a horizontal rectangular wing was added to the edifice; in 1626 Bishop Baldassare Cagliares added a recess at the back and in 1679 Bishop Molina laid the first stone of the choir which was inaugurated on 28 June 1682. The terrible earthquake of 11 January 1693 destroyed the old Cathedral almost completely except for the sacristy and the newly constructed choir. The latter had already been decorated with a fine altarpiece, a canvas representing St Paul's Conversion and a fresco depicting St Paul's Shipwreck as well as five other canvases, all painted by Mattia Preti (1613-1699). These fortunately survived the earthquake. The reconstruction of a larger Cathedral in the new baroque style was immediately taken in hand and entrusted to the Maltese architect Lorenzo Gafa' who eleven years before had constructed the apsed choir. There was no need for a new plan: Gafa' had previously submitted the plan and wooden model for a church in the new baroque style and the Cathedral Chapter had examined and approved them on 18 May 1692, that is eight months before the earthquake had taken place. The new Cathedral was completed and consecrated in October 1702 by Bishop Cocco Palmieri (1684-1713) whose coat-of-arms along with those of the reigning Grand Master Fra Ramon Perellos (1697-1720) and of the City of Medina were placed on the façade over the main entrance.

Below: Aerial view of the Cathedral.
Opposite: View of interior.

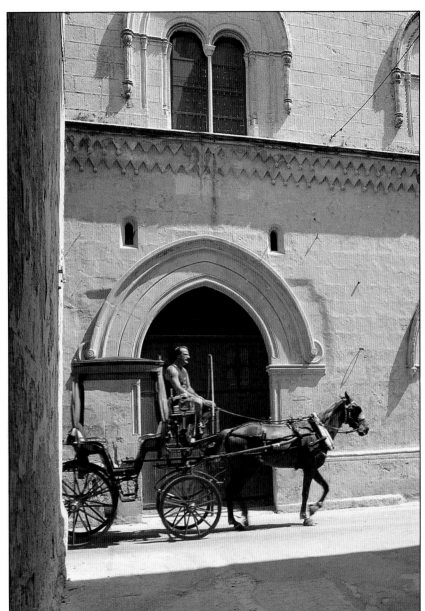

Palazzo Falzon (Norman House).

Among the attractions of Mdina are the numerous and varied door-shutters, both ancient and more recent, which can be seen in the doorways of mansions and houses in the town.

GOZO

21

90,91
Zebbug

Marsalforn

21

Ir-Ramla

San Blas Bay

42 Ramla Bay

Ta'Pinu
61,91

Gharb
2,91

Ghasri
90,91

Xaghra
64,65

San Lawrenz 2,91

Is-Srug

Nadur
42,43

Qala
42,43

Victoria
terminus

Dwejra Bay

Santa
Lucija
14

Kercem

14

Xewkija

42,43

Ghanjsielem
42,43

Car ferry Mgarr-Sliema

Mgarr
25

COMINO

Munxar
50

Xlendi
87

Sannat

50

Car ferry Mgarr-Marfa

Armier
50

Marfa & Cirkewwa
45,452,453

Paradise
Bay

48 to Bugibba/Qawra via Ghadira

Mellieha Bay

Biskra

Ghadira
44

Anchor Bay

Mellieha
43

Xemx

to Ra
(summe

Manikata

Ghajn Tuffieha
47,52

Golden Bay

51 to Bugiba/Qawra

Ghajn Tuffieh
Bay

Mgarr
47

Ta'l-Abatija

Tas-Santi

N

49 to Ghajin Tuffieha
48 to Cirkewwa via Ghadira
51 to Sliema ferry via Coast Road
70 to Rabat via Mosta and Ta'Qali
86
427 to Marsaxlokk

to Bugiba Qawra via Coast Road
to Rabat via St.Julians, Taz-Zwejt,
Mosta and Ta'Qali

Car ferry Mgarr-Sliema

Car ferry Valletta-Sicillia

Bahar
68 ic-Caghaq

St.Andrews
67,671
672

St.Julian's/Paceville

Gharghur
55

Naxxar
54,56

Ta'Giorni 66 Sliema 60 61
San Gwann 62 ★ 70

Mosta
53,57

Taz-Zwejt Gzira

Lija

Birkirkara
71,78
Balzan 41,42

VALLETTA
terminus

Ferry
Floriana Vittoriosa Kalkara
4
1,2,6 Xghajra
23 to Cospicua

40
Corinthia
Palace 74
San Anton
Gardens

Msida/Pieta

75 St.Lukes
Hospital
3 Senglea Cospicua
22 to Marsascala
23 to Xghajra
28 to Zejtun

San
Leonardo

Ta'Qali

St. Venera

Hamrun

Attard

Qormi
90,91

Marsa

18,21 Zabbar

Mdina
65
81

M A L T A

Paola

Fgura

Tarxien

Marsaskala
19
22 to Cospicua

65 to Sliema ferry via Ta'Qali, Mosta,
80 Taz-Zwejt and St.Julian's
83 to Xemxija
86 to Bugiba via Mosta and Ta'Qali

Zebbug
88

St.Vincent
de Paule

37

Luqa
36
15
Santa Lucia

Zejtun
26,29
28 to Cospicua

St.Thomas
Bay
29

St. Thomas Bay

Siggiewi
89
94 to Ghar Lapsi
(summer only)

LUQA AIRPORT

8 Gudja&
Ghaxaq

Buskett

Mqabba
Kirkop

Marsaxlokk
27
427 to Bugiba

Qrendi
35

Safi

Birzebbuga
11,115

Marsaxlokk
Bay

Ghar Lapsi
94

to Siggiewi
(summer only)

32,34,39
Zurrieq

Hal Far
13

Kalafrana
12